0 9 MAY 2024

Gill Hek and Pam Moule

THIRD EDITION

Making Sense of RESEARCH

An Introduction
for Health
and Social Care
Practitioners

SAGE Publications

Los Angeles • London • New Delhi • Singapore

© Gill Hek and Pam Moule 2006

First edition published by Continuum in 1996
Second edition published by Continuum in 2002
Reprinted by SAGE Publications 2003
This third edition published 2006
Reprinted 2007

Apart from any fair dealing for the purposes of research
or private study, or criticism or review, as permitted
under the Copyright, Designs and Patents Act, 1988, this
publication may be reproduced, stored or transmitted
in any form, or by any means, only with the prior
permission in writing of the publishers, or in the case
of reprographic reproduction, in accordance with the
terms of licences issued by the Copyright Licensing
Agency. Enquiries concerning reproduction outside those
terms should be sent to the publishers.

SAGE Publications Ltd
1 Oliver's Yard
55 City Road
London EC1Y 1SP

SAGE Publications Inc.
2455 Teller Road
Thousand Oaks, California 91320

SAGE Publications India Pvt Ltd
B 1/I 1 Mohan Cooperative Industrial Area
Mathura Road, New Delhi 110 044
India

SAGE Publications Asia-Pacific Pte Ltd
33 Pekin Street #02-01
Far East Square
Singapore 048763

British Library Cataloguing in Publication data

A catalogue record for this book is available
from the British Library

ISBN 978-1-4129-2361-3
ISBN 978-1-4129-2362-0 (pbk)

Library of Congress Control Number available

Typeset by C&M Digitals (P) Ltd., Chennai, India
Printed on paper from sustainable resources
Printed in Great Britain by The Cromwell Press Ltd, Trowbridge, Wiltshire

Contents

Figures

Tables

Preface

This book is intended for qualified health and social care practitioners and students who have not had any opportunity to study or experience research. It is a basic introductory text designed to be of practical use for the practitioner of today. Our aim is to 'demystify' and explain research by introducing the essential elements relevant to the health and social care professions.

The idea and motivation for the book came from our experience of teaching research awareness to pre-registration students and qualified practitioners on various courses. We were very aware of the need to make the topic of research as interesting as possible and this included making it relevant for practice. This book is clearly aimed at giving qualified health and social care practitioners and students an introduction to research with the expectation that those practitioners wanting to 'do' research, will gain research training and read more in-depth and definitive texts to help them.

This third edition includes as its readership within the health and therapy professions, physiotherapists, radiographers, occupational therapists, podiatrists, speech and language therapists, midwives and nurses. Within social care, we have mainly directed the text at social workers and social work students as the primary group concerned with professional practice and decision-making across a range of social care tasks. We have considered statutory, voluntary and non-profit health and social services across primary, community, hospital and residential care.

We have closely examined policy documents particularly related to the modernisation agendas in health and social care and we take the view that health and social care practitioners need to be 'research literate'. We introduce concepts such as 'evidence-based practice' and some of the issues and challenges faced by practitioners. We provide a foundation for developing research knowledge and a basis for the critical appraisal of research. Through this knowledge, we hope to help practitioners make sense of it all and enable them to become 'critical consumers of research'. This in turn will empower them to provide the highest standards of care for their patients and clients.

The layout of the book is straightforward and each chapter can be read on its own without the need to continually refer to other chapters. Following the first chapter that provides an overview of evidence-based practice and research in practice, and Chapter 2 that discusses the nature of knowledge, Chapters 3–9 explore the research process in some detail. Chapter 10 considers the often neglected area of ethics in research, and Chapter 11 is a key chapter that considers critical appraisal of research. The final chapter looks at the complex issues related to the dissemination and implementation of research into practice.

We have provided three appendices that we hope will be useful resources for practitioners, and a glossary that defines appropriate research terms. Each chapter has learning outcomes, key terms and a list of suggested further reading. References to publications referred to in each chapter will be found towards the end of the book.

We hope that this book will make research interesting for practitioners, and that it will stimulate further exploration of the subject. More importantly, our desire is to see practitioners understand and 'make sense of research' so that they can consider it in their daily practice. Clients and patients can benefit from practitioners who are able to use research appropriately, and provide the highest standards of care possible. This is our ultimate aim.

Acknowledgements

In this third edition of *Making Sense of Research* we would like to acknowledge the major contribution made by Maggie Judd to the previous editions, and wish her well in her new work. Our grateful thanks go to the health and social care students from our university who have undoubtedly made us think carefully, and justify the importance of why practitioners need an understanding of research. We recognise the influence of the many qualified health and social care professionals in local health and social services and voluntary sector organisations who have attended various 'research awareness' courses organised by us. They have prevented us from making research awareness an 'academic exercise' by keeping our feet firmly rooted in practice and challenging any assumptions we might make about evidence-based practice in the 'real' world.

We remain grateful to our colleagues in nursing, social work, physiotherapy, radiography, podiatry, midwifery and occupational therapy who have provided us with real examples that are of direct relevance to health and social care professionals today. Finally, we would like to thank our families who have, as usual, supported us as we worked on this third edition.

1 The Role of Research in the Health and Social Care Professions

Learning Outcomes

On completion of this chapter the reader should be able to:

- understand the development of research in the health and social care professions
- appreciate the need to become 'research literate'
- identify the major factors that contribute to debates about the nature of research and evidence
- understand the emergence and development of evidence-based practice
- consider different ways of defining research.

Key Terms

- research literacy ■ research capacity and capability
- evidence-based practice ■ definitions of research ■ research in context ■ hierarchies of evidence

Introduction

The term 'research literate' or 'research aware' has been used by many to describe the way that the professional health and social care practitioner should be in the twenty-first century. This is a term that we favour as our intention in this introductory book is not to provide a text that equips health and social care professionals to undertake research, but rather to assist all practitioners to become research literate or research aware through a greater understanding of research within their respective professional groups. However, this does not mean that we think health and social care practitioners should not be undertaking research. To the contrary, health and social care professions all need more researchers in their field of practice and it is important to build the research capability (skills) of practitioner researchers as well as research capacity (volume). However, we believe that particular skills and knowledge are required to become a researcher in a particular field of practice, such as social work, midwifery, physiotherapy, nursing, just as in any other specialist area, such as mental health, child protection, cancer care, and that is beyond the remit of this book.

The majority of health and social care practitioners do not have, nor necessarily need, the skills required to undertake a research project themselves. What we all need, however, are the skills and knowledge to appreciate, understand and use research and evidence in order to provide the highest quality and most effective care possible for our patients, clients and service users. It should be a natural activity for health and social care practitioners to keep up to date and use research findings and evidence in their work, and being 'research literate' is one of the basic skills required of all these professional groups.

Research literacy

By using the term 'research literate' we mean: having the capability for critical thought, possessing analytical skills, having the skills to gain access to relevant research and evidence, having a critical understanding of research processes, and being able to read and critically appraise research and other types of evidence. Through possessing these skills and being research literate, health and social care practitioners will be able to assess the appropriateness of using specific evidence in their daily practice, and identify research problems and priorities. This is not an easy task and it is generally accepted that more nurses need to become research aware and research literate.

Health and social care practitioners also need to have an awareness of any potential ethical issues that may arise in relation to their patients, clients and service users if research is undertaken. This includes having an understanding of the implications of collecting data for other researchers, and the statutory duties and responsibilities associated with their professional groups that may not sit comfortably with research.

The groups that fall within the scope of health care and therapy professions that we have included in this book are nurses, midwives, physiotherapists, podiatrists, occupational therapists, speech and language therapists, and radiographers. Within social care we are mainly considering social workers as the primary group concerned with skilled professional practice and decision-making across a range of social care tasks (Macdonald, 2000). These health and social care professional groups span: hospital, residential, community and primary care; statutory, voluntary, independent and non-profit health and social services; and preventative, therapeutic and supportive services.

Prior to the introduction of diploma and graduate level pre-qualifying education for many of these professional groups in health and social care, research awareness and understanding were limited in the curriculum. This means that there are many qualified practitioners who have not had the opportunity to explore and become aware of research and **evidence-based practice**. These practitioners now recognise the need to become research literate and are seeking out opportunities to develop their understanding and awareness of research in the health and social services. There are many courses, study days, online and web-based resources, books and journal articles which are more accessible to most practitioners, and being able to attend a conference or specialised study day is also a good opportunity to become aware of research in one's own area of practice.

The care provided by all health and social care practitioners must be based on current knowledge and evidence that promotes the delivery of the highest standards of care possible. All the professional groups in health and social care are working hard to develop their own professional knowledge base with strong foundations built on research and evidence. Each professional group has research leaders who are striving to develop research knowledge and evidence for both their professional colleagues and the users of their services, such as clients and patients. Excellence in practice is dependent on the research and evidence base of each professional group and we all have a responsibility in some way to contribute to our own profession's knowledge through research.

Researchers in health and social care

As previously mentioned, there are many people who undertake research that could come under the broad category of health and social care research. There are those in disciplines such as psychology, sociology, social and welfare policy, and other social sciences who have a clear relationship with health and social care and who research from the perspective of their own discipline using techniques that might be specifically related to that discipline. There are also researchers, such as historians, economists, statisticians, epidemiologists, geographers and anthropologists, who will again bring their own discipline to a particular research project. There are also practitioners who undertake research from their own professional perspective, such as physiotherapy, social work, nursing, in order to make a direct improvement to their practice and this may involve more active research approaches than in other areas of research. Practitioners who are working in therapy or nurse consultant roles, or those who are advanced practitioners, are also likely to be undertaking research directly related to their area of expertise. There is also a growing body of patient or client-led research that brings a different perspective to the research endeavour. Working in multi-disciplinary teams, this type of research and the researchers on the team will be seeking to directly improve care within a particular client or patient group.

The growing area of health services research is likely to involve multi-disciplinary teams including health professionals, social scientists, statisticians and health economists. There may be physiotherapists, nurses, podiatrists or speech and language therapists directly employed in specialities, such as carer support, breast care, respiratory medicine, paediatrics, diabetes care, who undertake small studies in their own area of work; or there may be health and social care practitioners employed directly onto a specific project, for example, a clinical trial examining the effectiveness of a counselling service, or looking at what works in family support or child protection. A quick look at journals related to the health and social services will give some idea of the types of research that are conducted and reported by health and social care professionals.

Some health and social care practitioners may undertake research as part of a pre- or post-qualifying degree course, or during a period of study, and many more now study at postgraduate level including doctoral studies. As previously mentioned, health and social care students studying at diploma level are often not encouraged to undertake research, although they might perform activities, such as designing a questionnaire or interviewing colleagues, as exercises to help them understand research methods. More commonly they will develop skills to enable them to critically appraise research in order to inform their practice. Students may also undertake project work or write essays using research findings and evidence. All these activities are important and necessary in helping health and social care practitioners to become research literate.

The development of evidence-based practice

Evidence-based practice has rapidly emerged since the early 1990s and has had a significant impact on health and social service provision. As the starting point for this movement, evidence-based medicine has become a 'cornerstone of UK health policy' (Reynolds, 2000), and there has been a swift adoption of key **concepts** in other professional groups particularly in nursing, physiotherapy, public health, mental health and child health (Trinder, 2000a). In other areas, such as social work, the notion of evidence-based practice has been subject to 'reworking' and re-interpretation within a framework of existing research and practice **traditions** (Trinder, 2000b).

The growth of evidence-based practice is not without its critics across all areas of health and social care, and there is limited consensus on the merits of evidence-based practice. Some point out that there is no 'evidence' that evidence-based practice actually works; that it constrains professional decision-making and autonomy; that it is too simple and is 'cook-book' practice; that it is a covert method of rationing resources; and that it exalts certain types of research evidence over other types of knowledge and evidence. Health and social care practitioners need to be aware of the debates surrounding evidence-based practice both within their own professional group and more generally in the health and social services (see Trinder, 2000c, for a useful critique).

The successful and rapid emergence of evidence-based practice has been argued by those within the movement as being due to the obvious, simple, sensible and rational idea 'that practice should be based on the most up-to-date, valid and reliable research' (Trinder, 2000a: 3). The context in which it has developed may go some way to explain why the movement has been flourishing in many areas of health and social care practice. Within recent years there has been a cultural shift within the health and social services from one of trusted professional judgement-based practice to that of evidence-based practice. Davies, Nutley and Smith (2000), Trinder (2000a) and others suggest that there are a number of contributing factors in the development of evidence-based practice including:

- growth in an increasingly well-educated and well-informed public
- increasing awareness of the limitations of science
- growth in consumer and self-help groups
- intensive media scrutiny
- explosion of the availability of different types of information and data
- developments in information technology
- increasing emphasis on productivity and competitiveness
- emphasis on 'value-for-money' audit
- increase in scrutiny, accountability and regulation of professional groups
- major adverse events within the health and social services
- lawsuits and compensation claims.

This cultural shift has resulted in an explosion of evidence-based initiatives and new terminology within the health and social services since the mid-1990s including:

- centres such as Evidence-based Mental Health, Evidence-based Nursing, Research in Practice for Adults, Social Care Institute for Excellence (SCIE)
- specialist 'evidence-based' journals
- websites and web-based discussion lists
- electronic bibliographic resources for evidence-based practice.

This has had an effect on how research and evidence are considered and used by current practitioners within health and social care and how evidence and practice drive (and are driven by) practice and policy more than ever before.

Within both the health and social services, political ideology plays a role in shaping both policy and practice. This can influence how health and social problems are perceived, problems solved, and services delivered by different professional groups. The professional groups work across organisations more than in the past, and joint working within and between many areas of health and social services means that communication and collaboration need to be effective if patients, clients and service users are to receive the highest quality of care. The development of public health services and the growing shift towards community and primary care have also had a role in the development of evidence-based initiatives. It is reasonable to say that the evidence-based practice movement has had an effect all through the health and social services including practice, policy, management, education, and includes all health and social care professionals who make decisions.

What is evidence-based practice?

There are three key components to evidence-based practice:

1   Best available current evidence.
2   Preferences of individual clients and patients.
3   Expertise and experience of the professional.

All three elements need to be used together, although the importance of each may vary in different situations. The overriding principle is that of giving the most effective care to maximise the quality of life for an individual, and, although describing evidence-based medicine, Sackett, Richardson, Rosenburg and Haynes point out that 'evidence-based medicine builds on and reinforces, but never replaces, clinical skills, clinical judgement and clinical experience' (1997: 5).

Evidence-based practice is seen as comprising five explicit steps:

1   Identify a problem from practice and turn it into a specific question. This might be about the most effective intervention for a particular client, or an assessment of causation, or about the most appropriate test, or about best method for delivering a service.
2   Find the best available evidence that relates to the specific question, usually by making a thorough search of the literature.

3 Appraise the evidence for its validity (closeness to the truth), usefulness (practical application) and methodological rigour.
4 Identify current best evidence and, together with the patient or client's preferences, apply it to the situation.
5 Evaluate the effect on the patient or client, and the practitioner's own performance.

Current pre-qualifying education will help students address all these stages. Specifically practitioners need to learn how to search effectively for appropriate evidence and research through a range of literature sources (see Chapter 4), and how to critically appraise research (see all chapters, but particularly Chapter 11 and Appendix 1).

What counts as evidence?

There are many debates and arguments across all the health and social care professions about what constitutes evidence. For the purposes of this book, we take the view that research (which we define later) is one form of evidence amongst many other types of evidence. Health and social care professionals should be aware of the debates surrounding types of evidence including research, and in particular hierarchies of evidence. The idea of a 'hierarchy of evidence' has evolved as a response to the notion that some research designs, particularly those using quantitative methods, are more able than others to provide robust evidence of effectiveness, that is, what works. The most common type of hierarchy (see Table 1.1) places randomised controlled trials at the top of the hierarchy.

Other chapters in this book guide the reader through some of these research designs, and the 'further reading' at the end of this chapter points to some useful texts that introduce the debates surrounding types and hierarchies of evidence. Of particular importance are the debates surrounding the role of experimentation and randomised controlled trials in social care, which, in health, have been seen as the 'gold standard' of research design for looking at effectiveness of interventions (see, for example, Davies et al., 2000; Trinder and Reynolds, 2000). As is evident later, hierarchies of evidence of effectiveness are only helpful for considering evidence about whether something *works*, such as a treatment, therapy, educational

Table 1.1   *A basic hierarchy of strength of evidence about effectiveness (what works)*

1 Evidence from a systematic review of multiple well-designed randomised controlled trials.
2 Evidence from one or more well-designed randomised trials.
3 Evidence from trials without randomisation or from single before-and-after studies, cohort, time series or matched case-controlled studies or observational studies.
4 Evidence from well-designed descriptive studies or qualitative research.
5 Opinions from expert committees or formal consensus methods.
6 Expert opinion.

See Gray (1999), Khan et al. (2003) and NHS Centre for Reviews and Dissemination (2001) for more detailed types of hierarchies of evidence.

programme. Evidence about how clients feel about something, or whether patients are satisfied, or the perspective of different types of practitioners, is best captured by different types of research and evidence that do not particularly feature in any type of hierarchy. Furthermore, as will be seen in Chapter 2, evidence can be based on different types of knowledge, of which some types are more robust and systematic than others.

Definitions of research

There are many ways of defining research ranging from very broad to narrow interpretations. A quick look through the literature would reveal many different definitions. A broad definition might suggest that research is any type of enquiry that generates knowledge and may include a variety of activities. Depoy and Gitlin (1994) favour a broad approach in their text that is concerned with health and human services research. They define research as:

> multiple, systematic strategies to generate knowledge about human behaviour, human experience, and human environments in which the thought and action process of the researcher are clearly specified so that they are logical, understandable, confirmable and useful. (p. 5)

This is an interesting definition in that the role of the researcher is acknowledged as important. Many definitions of research do not consider this aspect. Polit and Beck (2006) describe research as a systematic examination that uses scientific methods to answer questions or solve problems. There is a clear practical dimension in that research is seen to answer questions or solve problems as in Burns' definition of 'a systematic investigation to find answers to a problem' (2000: 3). As with the Depoy and Gitlin (1994) definition, 'systematic' is a common theme and one that occurs in many other definitions.

The health and social care professions are clearly linked with the social sciences and one definition of social research by Neuman (1994) may be of use:

> Social research involves many things. It is how a person finds out something new and original about the social world. To do this, a researcher needs to think logically, follow rules, and repeat steps over and over. A researcher will combine theories or ideas with facts in a systematic way and use his or her imagination and creativity. (p. 2)

Blaxter, Hughes and Tight focus on the nature of research and 'types' of research, such as pure, applied, strategic, basic, market, evaluation, exploratory, collaborative, action, descriptive, which can be found in an enormous range of research methods books. However, they point out that the basic characteristics shared by all is 'that they are, or aim to be, planned, cautious, systematic, and reliable ways of finding out or deepening understanding' (1996: 5).

For the purpose of this book, we define research as:

> a systematic approach to gathering information for the purposes of answering questions and solving problems in the pursuit of creating new knowledge about health and social care.

The definition is broad in order to encompass all aspects of health and social care and it recognises the systematic nature of collecting data. In addition, we consider the active, practical and applied nature of health and social care practice. In order to distinguish research from audit and development work, which are closely related, we define research as creating new knowledge.

No single definition will be satisfactory, however, and in order to be able to understand research at an introductory level, we feel that a working definition might be helpful. Chapter 2 considers how the research and evidence used in decision-making by practitioners is informed by different types of knowledge available to the practitioners.

Key Points

- All health and social care practitioners need to become 'research literate'.
- 'Research literacy' includes the skills and knowledge to appreciate, understand and use research.
- Not all health and social care practitioners should be conducting research as part of their daily work or professional development.
- Health and social care practitioners need to consider the tensions and conflict associated with the concept of evidence-based practice.
- There are many definitions of research with most incorporating a view about the search for knowledge through a systematic and rigorous process.
- Health and social care practitioners need to become critical consumers of research to enable them to provide excellence in care.

Further Reading

Brown, B., Crawford, P. and Hicks, C. (2003). *Evidence-based research: dilemmas and debates in health care*. Maidenhead: Open University Press.

Carnwell, R. (2000). Essential differences between research and evidence-based practice. *Nurse Researcher, 8* (2), 55–68.

Davies, H.T.O., Nutley, S.M. and Smith, P. (Eds.) (2000). *What Works? Evidence-based policy and practice in public services*. Bristol: The Policy Press.

Freshwater, D. and Bishop, V. (Eds.) (2004). *Nursing research in context*. Basingstoke: Palgrave Macmillan.

Goding, L. and Edwards, K. (2002). Evidence-based practice. *Nurse Researcher, 9* (4), 45–57.

Gomm, R. and Davies, C. (Eds.) (2000). *Using evidence in health and social care*. London: Sage.

Gray, J.A.M. (2003). *Evidence-based healthcare: how to make health policy and management decisions*. London: Churchill Livingstone.

Trinder, L. and Reynolds, S. (Eds.) (2000). *Evidence-based practice: a critical appraisal*. Oxford: Blackwell Science.

2 The Nature of Knowledge in Health and Social Care

Learning Outcomes

On completion of this chapter the reader should be able to:

- identify the sources of knowledge available to the health and social care professions
- appreciate the importance of research and evidence-based knowledge for health and social care practice.

Key Terms

- sources of knowledge ■ traditions ■ trial and error
- authority ■ scientific knowledge ■ tacit knowledge
- rituals ■ intuition ■ common sense ■ reflective practice

Introduction

Within this text we consider the development of knowledge and practice, and the significance of research and evidence-based information to the nature of knowledge. It is the intention of this chapter to consider how health and social care knowledge has developed, and to highlight the need for the health and social care professions to develop information as part of professional growth.

In an attempt to understand the nature of health and social care knowledge, the complexity of health and social care information is discussed and the multidimensional aspects of the profession's **theory** base are considered. The chapter will consider the importance of evidence-based practice, as identified in Chapter 1, specifically exploring the development of knowledge through tradition, ritualistic practice, **intuition, tacit knowledge, common sense**, authority, **trial and error**, and from a scientific base. Such discussions will reveal the many dimensions of health and social care theory, and, whilst not denigrating the development of any particular source of knowledge, will demonstrate the need for health and social care practice to question its knowledge base and accept those sources that provide a credible evidence base for practice. Thus, the practitioner might access a variety of forms of best evidence on which to base practice.

Traditions and rituals

'We do it this way because we believe this is the best way.' 'We do it the way the team leader likes it.' 'Dr X likes his patients to be treated in this particular way.' These statements reflect the use of tradition in the health and social care professions, the development of practice based on beliefs or myths which are accepted by the profession as a base for practice. Traditions can become customs, applied without critical thought, in a ritualistic way.

Walsh and Ford (1989, 1994) have devoted two texts to the discussion of ritual practices in nursing, which are full of examples of care being given without thought for individual need. These texts give a picture of the way in which traditions and **rituals** can impinge on all aspects of the patient's day and demonstrate the use of outdated practice by many nursing staff. It should be noted, however, that these texts are over a decade old and the absence of any new writing perhaps suggests a change in the ways in which traditional and ritualistic knowledge is being used to support health and social care practice.

Certain routine practices, which might be seen as ritualistic, are not necessarily undesirable. The performance of the handing over of client information from one staff member to another might be part of the care routine, but can also act as a vehicle for social exchange and enhances social cohesion and team working.

Whilst some ritualistic practices might be beneficial, it is vital that outdated and unsafe practices are identified to allow health and social care practitioners to feel confident in the delivery of safe practice. These practitioners cannot afford to perpetuate traditional and ritualistic practice if it is at the expense of developments that are beneficial to the patient and the profession. Professionals are accountable for their practice and must be able to identify that the best possible care is being made available so that practice can be justified as the most appropriate.

Intuition and tacit knowledge

The use of intuition and tacit knowledge is apparent in health and social care practice, but they cannot easily be explained. For example, the physiotherapist who knows what the patient's needs are without detailed assessment, the nurse who knows when a patient's life is at an end but cannot explain why this is known, uses intuitive and tacit knowledge. Intuition is perhaps having acute sensitivity, a sixth sense (Burnard, 1989), built on knowledge and experience, which is applied to decision-making and problem-solving. Tacit knowledge is developed through the experience accumulated from practice over a period of time. It is the development of 'expert opinion' that is a synthesis of formal knowledge and clinical expertise. It is suggested that much of this knowledge is passed on to future generations of practitioners through modelling of actions, tasks and attitudes (Gunilla, Drew, Dahlberg and Lutzen, 2002).

The lack of objectivity and ability to identify a rationale behind intuitive and tacit decisions has affected the recognition of this source of knowledge, preventing it being viewed as a valid **phenomenon** for scientific investigation. Yet, it is argued that there are many situations where the application of intuitive and tacit knowledge is essential. These include the management of ethical dilemmas and situations where there is inadequate information with which to interpret potential behavioural response (Rew and Sparrow, 1987). Debates surrounding the use of tacit and intuitive knowledge in nursing practice are growing (Welsh and Lyons, 2001; Gunilla et al., 2002; Whitehead, 2005).

The experienced health and social care professional brings additional sensitivity into practice. This use of intuition and tacit knowledge enables the delivery of the best possible care. Within nursing, Benner (1984) sees the experienced nurse as the expert clinician that uses intuition and tacit knowledge as part of delivering holistic (total) care to the patient. Benner (1984) suggests 'know how' knowledge, which highlights the difference between the beginner or novice and the expert practitioner, should be valued more highly. The development of 'knowledge that' into 'knowledge how' as part of acquiring intuition allows the expert practitioner to view the complete situation and therefore apply holistic care, using past experience and knowledge. The value of intuition to holistic care is discussed by Agan (1987) who links intuitive knowledge to the development of personal knowledge through **reflective practice**.

Problem-solving through reflective practice was popularised by Argyris and Schon (1974), with the more recent work of Schon (1987) suggesting the development of two types of reflective skill. Reflection-in-action, where the practitioner is appraising care and making changes at the time, is compared with reflection-on-action, which follows the event and uses an analysis of preceding practice to shape the future.

The work of Schon (1987) has been influential in health and social care practice and education. Though the work has been criticised (Greenwood, 1993), the value given to reflective practice in building personal knowledge, and ultimately in developing intuition and tacit knowledge, confirms the place of such knowledge in supporting health and social care practice.

Common sense

To use the words common sense is to suggest that something is widely accepted or generally known, as well as being logically reasoned and thought through. Sensible people would usually apply common sense. Knowledge based on common sense is therefore gained through accepted understanding, developed through individual experience that is not associated with any formal education or training.

Its value as a source of health and social care knowledge on which to base care can be limited, as can be seen through the examination of a common sense approach to certain clinical practices. Common sense might lead to covering a warm but shivering child with extra blankets. Learned knowledge of the need to reduce a child's temperature and therefore the shivering will result in the removal of any extra blankets and clothing. People often refer to childcare generally as common sense. The ability of parents to 'bring up' children will be evaluated through the amount of common sense the parents are thought to have. 'Mr and Mrs Smith will be "good" parents because they have a lot of common sense.' While it may be true that Mr and Mrs Smith will be 'good' parents, there is nothing that is at all common about the approach to parenthood. This can be seen in the plethora of texts available for parents that offer differing advice on all aspects of childcare.

As common sense is derived from individual experience, it is naturally limited, can be **biased**, and is drawn from individual reasoning rather than from external sources. The rationale for practice is consequently unsupported and may lead to the delivery of care that is not the best available, or the most appropriate.

Challenging practice based on common sense can be fraught with problems, as for the individual the practice is reasonable and understandable, and to them it makes common sense. Questioning common sense is, however, necessary to ensure care is of a high standard, and to prevent the perpetuation of practices that are restricted by individual experience and bias.

Common sense can provide a useful approach to care delivery, but health and social care professionals, as accountable practitioners, must critically examine and evaluate practice, choosing a knowledge base which supports professional and quality care.

Trial and error

Most of us use trial and error in solving problems on a day-to-day basis. When presented with a problem we will try one way of resolving it, and if this fails, different approaches will be taken until a solution is found. The solution is then remembered and used if the same or a similar problem occurs again.

Trial and error will only provide a solution to one specific problem and is therefore limited in its use. It is, however, an important source of knowledge, as others may recommend solutions for use when faced with similar problems. For example, much advice is offered to people with common colds, such as to take high doses of vitamin C, and stay in the warm. The implications of passing on knowledge gained through trial and error learning may be to contribute to traditional knowledge or in fact to authoritative knowledge that is considered later. Knowledge based on trial and error, which may ultimately be developed into traditional or authoritative knowledge, can provide a valid basis for care.

Authority

Knowledge originating from people in positions of authority, who are often perceived as experts, can be accepted as a reasonable basis for practice. There are many individuals who impart authoritative knowledge: specialist practitioners, senior managers, lecturers, medical staff, therapists. In fact all personnel in the health and social care environments have the potential to be seen as an authority. This may develop from the person's position, which is likely to be one of power, or the person's perceived knowledge and experience, or the very personality and self-portrayal of the individual.

As a source of knowledge, the expert may have much to offer that will benefit students, staff and ultimately patients. There is, however, a concern that the expert will not be challenged, that the position of authority is above reproach and that the knowledge of the expert can be used without questioning the source. It is possible for the expert to offer a vehicle for the perpetuation of traditional and ritualistic practice, of practices which support the expert's preferences and idiosyncrasies, rather than practice which is in fact sound and based on fact. There are many examples of such practice. The teaching of cardio-pulmonary resuscitation has varied according to the individual demonstrating basic life support skills, and continues to vary despite the development of Resuscitation Council UK Guidelines (2005) that are based on the current evidence base. It is therefore important for the recipient of authoritative knowledge to establish the original source of the information and determine a basis for practice that is justifiable.

It should also be remembered that experts impart knowledge through publication. The content of any journal article or text should not be accepted as true just because it is published, but it should be questioned and critically appraised. All health and social care professionals need critical reading skills to determine the strengths and weaknesses of published work, and should be encouraged to adopt a questioning approach (see Chapter 11).

Policies and procedures are also used to guide practice. Many procedures used in the past gave step-by-step instructions for the practitioner to follow. More recently, the procedural approach has been succeeded by sound principles. These are less prescriptive and offer guidelines for safe practice. It is, however, important that the knowledge behind clinical principles is established. Rationales should be offered, which include referenced facts and high-quality evidence.

Scientific knowledge

Scientific knowledge is seen as informing health and social care practice through solving problems in a logical, systematic and rigorous way. The scientific approach to generating knowledge is seen as organised, following a series of logical steps (Polit and Beck, 2006). Chapter 1 gave some of the many definitions of research, which share commonality in suggesting a systematic approach to testing and generating knowledge. This suggests that the research process, described in Chapter 3, is used to provide a logical and systematic structure to problem-solving.

The need for scientific knowledge is acknowledged in the opening chapter, as is the need for education and training to enable health and social care practitioners to develop research awareness skills. Such skills are necessary to critically analyse and appraise research, thus allowing the identification of strengths and weaknesses in the research process (See Chapter 11).

The need for the health and social care professions to develop a scientific knowledge base for practice is also established, with research being viewed as a professional necessity. It is vital that the accountable practitioner can confidently deliver care based on reliable research evidence. There are benefits for the patient and professions in developing research-based health and social care practice.

The development of scientific knowledge in health and social care has its difficulties and limitations. Just as health and social care professionals need to be critical in their appraisal of other **sources of knowledge**, so they need to be critical of research. The strengths and weaknesses of scientific knowledge must be identified through **critical appraisal**, as is highlighted in Chapter 11.

One independent organisation supporting practitioners in the development of evidence-based treatment is the National Institute for Health and Clinical Excellence (NICE). NICE is responsible for providing national guidelines in the promotion of good health and the prevention and treatment of ill health. NICE provides guidance in three areas for the National Health Service in England and Wales: public health, health technologies (medicines and treatments) and clinical practice (see http://www.nice.org.uk).

All research is fallible, all will have both strengths and limitations that should be considered in evaluating any of the recommendations made for practice.

The very nature of health and social care practice causes research difficulties, including ethical problems and measurement issues. Certain research may not gain ethical approval. For example, delaying pressure area risk assessment for more than six hours following admission to hospital ignores current best practice recommendations (NICE, 2003) and could endanger participants. Such research would be seen as negligent and unethical.

Though there are many measurement tools available to the researcher (see Chapter 8), the collection of quality information, as part of a qualitative approach, poses difficulties. The measurement of, for example, opinions, feelings, thoughts, viewpoint, behaviour, can challenge research.

Additional difficulties lie in health and social care itself. The impetus for research can be uncertain, the education and research skills of the professions are still developing, and the application of research knowledge to practice is not always uniform.

Health and social care professionals need to acquire research knowledge and skills, to shape the future of professional research. These skills are now developed to a basic level within all pre-registration courses, which often require the completion of a research critique, research project or dissertation. Most post-registration courses include research awareness skills and there are specialised research courses at master's level, with increasing opportunities for doctoral level studies. Career pathways are also developing for those professionals who choose to make a career in research and practice or education.

Scientific knowledge may not always be the most appropriate source of information on which to base practice, but the use of scientific enquiry can establish the basis for care. It should be remembered that all types of knowledge discussed in this chapter can provide a basis for health and social care practice and the type of knowledge base employed may change with time and context as there is no single permanent truth.

Key Points

- Health and social care professionals need to be aware of the concept of evidence-based practice.
- The development of health and social care theory has been multidimensional, with knowledge being generated from many sources.
- Research must support measurement and the testing of knowledge in a systematic way.
- The professions are still developing research skills and expertise.

Further Reading

Brown, B., Crawford, P. and Hicks, C. (2003). *Evidence-based research: dilemmas and debates in healthcare.* Maidenhead: Open University Press.

Davies, M. (2005). *Evidence-based practice: a primer for healthcare professionals.* Edinburgh: Elsevier Churchill Livingstone.

Meuler, R. (2005). *Issues of evidence-based practice in medicine and healthcare: a discussion of the ethical issues.* Berlin: Springer-Verlag.

Pawson, R. (2003). *Types of quality of knowledge in social care.* London: Social Care Institute for Excellence.

Rolfe, G. (1998). *Expanding nursing knowledge: understanding and researching your own practice.* Oxford: Butterworth Heinemann.

Walter, I. (2004) *Improving the use of research in social care practice.* London: Social Care Institute for Excellence.

3 Overview of the Research Process

Learning Outcomes

On completion of this chapter the reader should be able to:

- identify the stages of the research process
- understand the inter-relationships between the stages of the research process
- appreciate how the research process guides research activity.

Key Terms

- research process ■ qualitative approach ■ quantitative approach

Introduction

This chapter offers a broad overview of the stages that comprise the research process, discusses the functions of the different processes, and highlights its use as a framework for research activity. In doing so, the chapter provides the basis to many of the chapters that follow, where issues raised will be further explored.

The research process is a framework which enables researchers to start with a research problem and follow a series of logical stages, to end with an outcome or result (see Table 3.1). It is a theoretical model which, when applied by researchers, may not be followed in a sequential way. It is more likely that some stages of the process would run concurrently, interrelate and interchange, and some may be completely omitted. For example, the **research question** may be formulated initially and then redefined or completely rewritten as the researcher has an opportunity to reflect on the progress of the research study.

In undertaking a research study, the researcher's progression through the research process would depend on the research approach taken, which can be qualitative (**inductive**) or quantitative (**deductive**). The outcomes of qualitative approaches are achieved without the use of statistical measures, although some do include some degree of statistical analysis (see Chapter 5). In contrast, the quantitative approach relies on statistical measures for its results and therefore necessitates the use of larger **samples** and more structured data collection tools (Polit and Beck, 2006).

Reflection by the researcher at each stage of the research process can be considered beneficial to the ultimate outcomes of the research. At each stage of the research process the researcher may make alterations to the continuation of the study based on progressive evaluations and thus hope to improve the final outcome and results.

Many writers, such as Bell (2005), consider the research process from an operational perspective. They discuss how to use the research process to write a research proposal (a plan of proposed work completed by a researcher prior to undertaking research). In particular, they describe how to plan and carry out a research project, and finally consider how to present the research findings.

For most health and social care professionals the research process provides a basis for evaluating and appraising completed research in a critical way, as is further discussed in Chapter 11. Knowledge of the stages of the research process therefore enables practitioners to read research reports. This is facilitated as researchers use the research process to structure the written presentation of research findings.

Identifying problems

The first stage in the research process is to define a problem. Health and social care professionals experiencing or observing

Table 3.1   Stages of the research process

- Identifying problems
- Searching the literature
- Critically reading research
- Research aims, questions and hypothesis
- Sampling techniques
- Data collection
- Data analysis
- Interpretation of results

a particular issue in their practice may generate the research problem at a local level. Research problems may also result from the identification of research priorities by, for example, the Department of Health which funds specific research studies into practice concerns, such as cancer or mental health. Charitable or private organisations such as Help the Aged, Joseph Rowntree Foundation, Mental Health Foundation and pharmaceutical companies may also fund research.

The researcher can be considering research problems that pertain to local, national or international issues, and may be working alone or as part of a research team. Whatever the scale of the research, the researcher must be clear about the relevance of researching the identified problem and have a clear understanding of the purpose of the research. In other words, what is the research trying to achieve, what are the outcomes hoping to show, and how will the outcomes be used?

Whatever the purpose of the research, the research problem needs to be researchable. The researcher needs to consider how the problem can be investigated, what type of results are likely to be generated and how they would be analysed. In addition, the researcher needs to address any ethical issues, such as whether patients, clients or staff are involved in the investigation.

The research problem is often broad and requires some refinement to form research aims, questions and **hypothesis** (see later discussions and Chapter 6). This is achieved by further exploration of the problem area, which includes searching and reading relevant literature.

Searching the literature

Having identified the research issue, the researcher must undertake a **literature search** before refining the problem. The literature search involves the retrieval of literature that is relevant to the research problem. The literature search should continue throughout the period of the research study to include any relevant literature published during the study period. However, the main literature search is likely to take place in the early stages of the research process.

The approach taken to searching the literature is important as this affects the breadth and depth of literature obtained. Different lines of enquiry may tempt the researcher as the search continues. The researcher must avoid diversions that have no relevance to the study. The literature search needs to be structured around key areas, perhaps starting with key concepts or words, and should progress systematically with the original research problem providing the continued focus for the search.

There are many aids to searching literature available that are fully discussed in Chapter 4. It is important that the researcher has sufficient knowledge and skills to access the resources. In addition, the researcher should use a reference or database system, recording details of literature that has been obtained, or is likely to be accessed during the study. These records will be used throughout the study and may be of use in the future, particularly if further research is undertaken.

As well as researchers, all health and social care professionals need to be able to undertake a literature search. Literature searching skills are important for professionals. Such skills will facilitate the development of practice, supporting the acquisition and updating of knowledge. This is essential for the development of evidence-based practice, and ultimately the quality of care. Professionals undertaking further courses will also need to use literature-searching skills to meet course work requirements.

Critically reading research

The reading of research literature often occurs concurrently with the literature search; however, the two stages are discussed separately to highlight fundamental differences between the two. The review of the research literature requires the use of critical appraisal skills, to determine the strengths and weaknesses of the research, whereas, the literature search is used to identify the literature for review.

The process of critical review requires knowledge of the research process and can be assisted by the use of a framework outlining the stages of critical appraisal (see Appendix 1). Critical reading skills used in the process of critical appraisal are discussed in Chapter 11. These skills are essential to the researcher and of importance to all health and social care professionals. If practice is to be developed from an objective research base, professionals must have the skills needed to analyse literature and offer an objective appraisal of research findings.

In reviewing the literature critically, the researcher may obtain the answer to the research problem negating the need for further research. Alternatively, the need for further research may be confirmed, and suggestions as to how the study should progress may be gained. For example, the research methodology could be replicated, or the data collection tool, such as a questionnaire, could, with the permission of the original researchers, be reproduced for use in the study.

Research aims, questions and hypothesis

The research aims, questions and hypothesis give focus and direction to the research study. The research aim, or aims, are generated, outlining what the research study is hoping to achieve. The research question is developed following the **literature review**, and narrows the original problem into a more concise statement.

The research hypothesis gives even greater focus to the research, as it offers a prediction of the anticipated research outcomes. The hypothesis is a statement that is tested by the researcher and, dependent on the findings, will either be accepted as true or rejected. Fuller explanations of this are given in Chapter 6.

Sampling techniques

Sampling involves the collection of information on which decisions can be made and conclusions drawn. The selection of a sample is therefore a very important part of the research process. Before a sample is selected the researcher identifies the target population, which includes the entire membership of the group in which the researcher is interested and from which information can be collected.

The **target population** could include participants or incidents. For example, the researcher may be interested in obtaining information from community physiotherapists. All community physiotherapists would therefore form the target population.

It is unlikely that the researcher would collect information from the entire target population, but a sample would be selected to take part in the study. The most important feature of sampling is the degree to which the sample represents the target population. For the sample to be truly representative, the participants need to reflect the target population in as many ways as possible. If the target population is student nurses following the adult branch, the sample needs to be made up of students in the adult branch. Limitation of difference between the target population and sample is achieved to some degree through the use of accepted sampling techniques.

Sampling techniques fall into two sampling strategies, **probability** and **non-probability sampling.** Probability sampling involves the use of random selection, with every member of the target population having an equal chance of being included in the sample. There are different probability sampling techniques including, simple, stratified, systematic and cluster sampling. Non-probability samples are selected without the use of random selection. The inclusion of subjects can be through convenience, quota, purposive and snowball sampling techniques. The different sampling techniques are discussed in Chapter 7.

Research design

The research design is a plan of how the research will proceed. It includes consideration of the research approach which is to be taken, and the research methods, data collection tools, and the methods of **data analysis** that are to be employed.

The research design might use quantitative (deductive) or qualitative (inductive) approaches to the research (see Chapter 5). This will be reflected in the sample size used, data collection method and techniques employed, and will be most evident in the results obtained and their analysis.

A **pilot study** is used as part of the research design, often to check sampling techniques, to test the **validity** and **reliability** of data collection tools. It also gives the researcher an opportunity to practise research skills, such as interviewing techniques.

The researcher will reflect on the experiences gained during the pilot study to refine aspects of the main study. This can provide financial benefits, and facilitate the effective use of resources in the final research study.

Data collection techniques

The researcher's choice of data collection instrument is influenced by the research approach taken. For example, a quantitative approach may use structured data collection techniques, such as a questionnaire; whereas, a qualitative approach may include the use of unstructured **interviews** or **observational** techniques.

The most commonly used data collection techniques include physiological and psychological measures, measuring scales, questionnaires, interviews, observations and documentary evidence (see Chapter 8).

Data analysis

The method of data analysis used will depend on the research approach taken and the techniques of data collection employed. To aid analysis, the results, often described as **raw data**, will be processed in some way.

Raw data generated through quantitative approaches tends to be numerical. Analysis of numerical data is often achieved using computer packages. Statistical tests are applied to the raw data to generate statistical results that are interpreted by the researcher (see Chapter 9).

Research that follows qualitative approaches generates data such as text, which is not amenable to statistical analysis. It is the content of the text that is important. The analysis may begin during the stage of data collection, and the researcher can begin to identify trends or themes whilst gathering information.

Interpretation of results

This stage of the research process includes interpretation of the results and the formulation of conclusions. Interpretation of the findings occurs in the light of the original research aims, questions and any hypothesis statements made, whilst reflecting on previous research studies identified in the critical review of the literature.

Discussions should highlight the researcher's interpretation of the results, acknowledge any limitations of the research process and consider the generalisability of the results (whether the results from the sample can be applied to a target population). The relevance and significance that the research findings might have for practice and further research would also be inferred from the research findings. For example, a change in existing practice may be recommended, or suggestions for further research may be made.

Presentation and dissemination

This final stage of the research process concentrates on the communication of the research findings to any sponsors or funding body and members of the health and social care professions, as well as to any participants, such as patients and clients. The research process is often used as a framework for presentation. **Dissemination** activity can occur at local, national and international levels. It might include the inclusion of a research dissertation at local trust or university libraries, or the presentation of the research as part of local research clubs and interest groups. Wider communication of the results can also be achieved through publication in national or international journals and the presentation of papers at a range of conferences. The internet web-pages and electronic media, such as electronic mail and discussion groups, can also provide a forum for dissemination.

Researchers hope that the research findings will increase the body of health and social care knowledge, and contribute to the improvement of practice. Further discussions on the dissemination of research are included in Chapter 12.

Key Points

- The research process is a framework that enables researchers to start with a problem and follow a series of logical and sequential steps, to end with an outcome or result.
- The research process includes the following stages: identifying the problems, searching the literature, critically reading research, setting research aims, questions and hypothesis, sampling techniques, data collection, data analysis and interpretation of results.
- Research problems can be generated locally or identified as research priorities by research funders, such as the government, or charitable organisations.
- Understanding the stages of the research process enables health and social care professionals to identify and read research studies.

Further Reading

Alston, M. and Bowles, W. (2003). *Research for social workers: an introduction to methods* (2nd ed.). London: Routledge.

Bowling, A. (2002). *Research methods in health: investigating health and health services* (2nd ed.). Buckingham: Open University Press.

Burns, R. (2000). *Introduction to research methods*. London: Sage.

Hicks, C. (1999). *Research methods for clinical therapists* (3rd ed.). Edinburgh: Churchill Livingstone.

Polit, D. and Beck, C. (2006). *Essentials of nursing research: methods, appraisal and utilization* (6th ed.). Philadelphia: Lippincott Williams and Wilkins.

Robson, C. (2002). *Real world research: a resource for social scientists and practitioner-researchers* (2nd ed.). Oxford: Blackwell.

4 Searching and Reviewing the Literature

Learning Outcomes

On completion of this chapter the reader should be able to:

- appreciate the need to develop literature searching skills
- define the term 'literature search'
- define the term 'literature review'
- identify sources of research and other forms of evidence
- identify the steps in undertaking a literature search
- understand the need to accurately record and store references.

Key Terms

■ literature search ■ literature review ■ internet ■ search strategy ■ abstract ■ electronic database ■ grey literature

---

Introduction

Finding and retrieving literature is an essential skill for all health and social care practitioners. As highlighted previously, it is essential that these professional groups become 'research literate' and this includes having the ability to search for, retrieve, and critically appraise all types of literature in their search for the best evidence. This chapter considers how to find

Table 4.1 *Reasons for a researcher to undertake a literature search*

- To see if the research question has already been answered.
- To become familiar and knowledgeable about other studies and relevant reports in a particular subject area.
- To gather ideas about appropriate research methodology for their own study, e.g. sample, methods, analysis.
- To see if there are similar studies which could be replicated or refined.
- To enable the researcher to become more focused.
- To assist the researcher in refining the research problem, subject or topic of interest into a clear and specific research question, aim or hypothesis.

and retrieve literature. This is commonly known as literature searching. The chapter will also consider literature reviewing in general terms, and Chapter 11 will consider the critical appraisal of different types of literature in some depth.

It is fairly obvious that researchers need to know their subject before embarking on a new piece of research. As Chapter 3 highlighted, in the early stages of the research process it is usual for a researcher to undertake a literature search at the commencement of a study (although with some research designs this does not come at the start). It is also important for the researcher to keep updating the search throughout the life of the study. The reasons for a researcher to undertake a literature search are multiple (see Table 4.1). They include developing a research proposal by getting ideas about methodology, checking that the work has not been undertaken before and extending the researcher's own knowledge about the subject.

The majority of health and social care practitioners are not going to be undertaking research themselves; however, they need to be able to undertake a literature search for a number of reasons (see Table 4.2). Any student embarking on a course today will need to quickly develop highly efficient and effective literature-searching skills. From pre-qualifying through to post-graduate and post-registration courses these skills will be in demand. Being able to search the literature effectively is also essential for evidence-based practice. Chapter 2 identifies ways in which we 'know' things, and points out that these are not always accurate or satisfactory. Finding literature to support or refute what we think we know is one way of developing our knowledge of a subject.

Table 4.2   *Reasons for a practitioner to undertake a literature search*

- To become familiar and knowledgeable about a particular subject.
- To keep abreast of new research and development in a particular subject area.
- As part of an academic assessment, coursework or project work.
- As necessary background work prior to setting standards and developing policy.
- As an important stage in any piece of research.
- As essential for developing professional knowledge and evidence-based practice.

The literature search

A literature search is a process by which a person looks for literature on a specific subject or topic. It needs to be undertaken in a systematic way, and requires time, determination and perseverance. There are a bewildering number of resources available that are constantly being developed, which makes it sometimes difficult to keep up. This chapter can only give a flavour of what is available today. With the 'explosion' of information to support evidence-based practice now available through new technology both the health and social services are attempting to make access to this information as easy as possible through a single point of access. The 'National Electronic Library for Health' and the National Institute for Social Work's 'Caredata' database are two initiatives that will soon enable free access to both practitioners and the public.

A number of steps can be followed, and it can be helpful for the 'novice' at literature searching to work through these (see Table 4.3). The first stage is to locate suitable libraries. Libraries situated in colleges and universities where there is a department related to one's professional group are likely to have the most useful resources. This will include computers for using catalogues, electronic databases and indexes, as well as access to the internet. There may also be libraries provided by local health and social services and other local libraries that may be useful. Students will have direct access to their university library and probably limited access to local health and social service libraries. Qualified staff are likely to have limited access to university libraries, which often have arrangements with local organisations in the health and social services. If a library provides a service in subjects such as psychology, biology, sociology, health, social policy, there will

Table 4.3   *Steps in undertaking a literature search*

- Locate suitable libraries with the necessary facilities to meet your needs.
- Become familiar with the variety of sources of literature.
- Become familiar with the range of 'searching facilities' available to you, e.g., electronic resources, indexes, abstracts and current awareness publications.
- Identify key words and develop a search strategy to help you methodically and thoroughly search through abstracts and indexes using CD-ROMs and the internet.
- Obtain the reports and articles which you want to critically appraise.
- Record the full details and reference of the article or report including the source.

be an even wider choice. Professional organisations, such as in nursing, social work and physiotherapy, may also provide services for supporting literature searching, for example, specific databases or article copying services.

Many people today have access to the internet either at home or through their place of work, and this will make searching easier although libraries will always be necessary for retrieving some literature. One really useful thing to do in the early stages is to use the introductory guides, workbooks and teaching sessions provided in most university libraries to enable you to get to grips quickly with the range of resources available. Libraries have changed over the past decade and librarians now teach the skills of information retrieval so that health and social care professionals can find information for themselves. Getting to know the librarians and support staff at the beginning of a literature search can also be very fruitful when things get hectic later on in the searching process!

Searching the literature

When the researcher has identified the resources available, the next stage is to become familiar with the variety of sources of literature (see Appendix 2). These can be loosely categorised into electronic sources such as: online databases; CD ROMs; internet resources such as discussion groups and gateways to sites; and printed sources such as card catalogues, indexes and **abstracts** in book format. There is also a huge range of organisations, resources and initiatives related to evidence-based practice and Needham (2000) provides a useful overview. Electronic searching facilities are generally more accessible and will be more up to date than printed sources and, once the skills have been mastered, are much quicker for searching as they have such comprehensive indexes.

Having become familiar with the range of resources available to search for literature, the researcher must now search through some of the most appropriate sources in a systematic and methodical manner using key words or terms. It is crucial to be clear about the question to which one is seeking an answer as a vague search for references to heart attack or child abuse will reveal thousands of potential references, most of which will not be relevant. The success of the search can be dependent on choosing the appropriate words and terms and developing a **'search strategy'** (see, for example, Hek, Langton and Blunden, 2000). If looking for evidence about 'what works?', a clear question with a number of components might include: type of patient or client; the problem or condition; the intervention or care; and an outcome. For example:

> Does a home-based teaching programme for parents of young children with hyperactivity disorder, improve parents' self-esteem and feelings of self-worth?

> How soon can patients who have swallowing difficulty following a stroke be safely fed orally?

Each of the components in the questions can be broken down into single words or terms that can then be combined in the search in order to produce only the most 'matched' references. Databases have thesaurus and subject headings to help identify different words to use; so, for instance, a search for a question about cancer might need to include words such as neoplasm and tumour and if it was an American database, alternative spellings might need to be used, for example, tumor. It is beyond this introductory text to go into depth about searching for literature and evidence, suffice to say that these skills are best learnt under the guidance of a librarian who will have extensive knowledge about the latest techniques and sources.

Other techniques that can be used for literature searching that are less effective, and probably best used in tandem with the main literature search, include: trawling through a few years (say the last ten) of a specialised journal, for example, *Nursing in Critical Care, British Journal of Occupational Therapy,*

Journal of Wound Care, Biomechanics, Pain, Issues in Social Work Education; 'snowballing' which means finding a few key articles particularly literature reviews, then chasing up relevant references from those articles to find others and so on until saturation; general searching on the internet and following up leads; and undertaking a broad search with vague terms, for example, child abuse, and then refining as you go along, rather than being specific right from the start.

Sources of literature

'Systematic reviews' are systematic collections of available literature on a topic, which have been critically appraised and reviewed and then published. They answer a specific question by summarising the available evidence and are an invaluable source, usually published by a team of systematic reviewers. Probably the most important sources of research literature are the academic and professional journals. Some journals contain original research articles, some contain summaries or systematic reviews of research, and many journals publish a mixture including case studies, discussion papers and news items. With the rise of evidence-based practice, there are now some really important journals that specialise in providing a review of research in a specific area, and often provide a commentary about the relevance for practice. They include: *Evidence-based Health Care, Evidence-based Mental Health, Effective Health Care,* and *Evidence-based Medicine.*

Books will only have limited use if the reader is looking for the very latest research. They are very useful for their coverage of a subject in some depth including research methodology; however, it usually takes a while to get a book published, so it may be a little out of date before it reaches the book shelves. This may not be important for some readers and for some subjects, but from a research and 'finding the latest evidence' point of view, usually the most recent work is necessary. Some edited books contain recent research on a particular topic, and these can be fairly up-to-date resources.

'Grey literature' includes reports, leaflets, bulletins, circulars and documents that may not be published in the conventional way and therefore not necessarily show up on electronic literature searches. A wide range of organisations may publish grey literature including: universities, voluntary organisations, independent research institutions, government departments, funders of research and professional organisations. Some reports might provide a really in-depth account of primary research, or an overview of research findings on a particular topic. Other types of literature might be policy statements, work-in-progress, theses, strategy documents, resource packs, all of which can be rich sources of information to supplement the main literature search.

Dealing with the literature

Once the references of the relevant articles and papers have been identified and noted from the various searches, they need to be obtained. In most libraries you can print out the articles you have found (particularly if the article is full text online) or find and photocopy the material you want, closely observing the copyright regulations. If the item is not available in the library, it may be possible for it to be ordered. When you have obtained the articles, books and papers you want, it is essential to make a full record of the details as it is so easy to forget them with so many items. This information will be needed when you write up or refer to the findings of your literature search. Details should include: full name of author(s); date of publication; article title/chapter title/book title/journal title; volume/issue; and page numbers. For books you also need the place of publication, the name of the publishers, edition number and names of editor(s). Some articles will contain all these details on the first page; however, for those that do not, it is useful to write these details on the front of the photocopied article. This will save a lot of wasted time later when you are trying to find the full details of the reference.

Storing references

It is very useful, and often necessary, to develop a system for storing the references that you obtain. This could be a simple card filing system with references recorded on separate cards and some form of index. Alternatively, you can develop a system on the computer that could easily be examined. Specific computer programmes for storing references can be purchased, for example, Reference Manager, Endnote Plus, and Procite, and these can be extremely useful as they allow you to use the stored references in different ways. For example, you can print out a list of your selected references in a variety of different styles such as the Harvard or Vancouver system. Another way of storing references on a computer is to use a database programme that is suitable for your computer. In your storage system you might also like to make notes on each item.

Literature review

A literature review is a written piece of work that examines and summarises a particular subject in some detail. It may be a large article or paper published as a 'literature review', or a shorter piece that is found at the beginning of a research article. A literature review may perform a number of functions. One function as a result of undertaking a literature search may be to summarise what is written about a particular subject or topic. This might be an uncritical summary that just describes what is written on a particular subject, or more importantly a systematic review which uses explicit, systematic and clearly identified methods to try to reach an unbiased conclusion. The techniques used in a systematic review include critical appraisal of each article or paper (see Chapter 11) and following strict criteria as part of the search strategy.

In order to undertake a critical literature review, the reviewer needs skills to undertake a comprehensive literature search (see above) as well as the skills of appraisal. Therefore, knowledge of research methods is essential as well as knowledge of the subject. Most academic assignments expect some critical appraisal of evidence, and for health and social care practitioners, a literature review may underpin the setting of standards or developing guidelines for good practice or for auditing purposes. For the researcher, a critical literature review is essential for informing the research approach and methods of investigating the research question. Reviewing the literature is an essential stage in any research process and Mason (1993) provides a very readable guide to the process of 'doing a literature review' (pp. 43–55).

Key Points

- All health and social care practitioners need to develop literature-searching skills.
- Searching for literature is a planned and methodical process with a number of key stages.
- There are numerous sources of literature including journals, reports and books.
- Indexes and abstracts can help locate relevant literature.
- Undertaking a thorough literature search requires time, energy and perseverance.

Further Reading

Clamp, C.G.L., Gough, S. and Land, L. (2004). *Resources for nursing research: an annotated bibliography* (4th ed.). London: Sage.

Gomm, R. and Davies, C. (Eds.) (2000). *Using evidence in health and social care.* London: Sage/Open University.

Hek, G., Langton, H. and Blunden, G. (2000). Systematically searching and reviewing literature. *Nurse Researcher, 7* (3), 40–57.

Khan, K., Kunz, R., Kleijnen, J. and Antes, G. (2003). *Systematic reviews to support evidence-based medicine.* London: The Royal Society of Medicine Press Ltd.

O'Dochartaigh, N. (2002). *The internet research handbook.* London: Sage.

Roberts, R. (1999). *Information for evidence-based care.* Abingdon: Radcliffe Medical Press.

Mistiaen, P., Poot, E., Hickox, S. and Wagner, C. (2004). The evidence for nursing interventions in the Cochrane Database of Systematic Reviews. *Nurse Researcher, 12* (2), 71–80.

5 Approaches to and Design of Research in Health and Social Care

Learning Outcomes

On completion of this chapter the reader should be able to:

- identify the difference between qualitative (inductive) and quantitative (deductive) approaches to research
- describe different approaches under the umbrella of inductive and deductive research
- appreciate how research designs such as action research and feminist research may be used as an agent of change and empowerment
- recognise the role played by systematic literature reviews to underpin professional practice.

Key Terms

- qualitative ■ systematic reviews ■ deductive ■ survey
- evaluation research ■ case studies ■ feminist research
- quantitative ■ inductive ■ mixed methods ■ experimental/
quasi-experimental ■ *ex post facto* ■ historical research
- action research

Introduction

There are many ways in which a researcher approaches the task of investigation. In the first instance a decision is made regarding the overall nature of the study, such as whether there is a theory to be tested (deductive research) or whether it is purely investigatory in which it is perceived that a theory will be developed (inductive).

Following on from that the researcher may choose a theoretical framework which will guide and underpin the whole of the study. Within health and social care this may be the use of a conceptual or philosophical framework, such as feminism or **phenomenology**, to give focus and direction to the study. Such approaches are now as familiar as the more traditional scientific, large scale surveys and **randomised controlled trials**. Crookes and Davies (1998) recognise the need for research to build on what is already known. They suggest that using a framework or frame of reference allows researchers to follow the thoughts of previous investigators. Furthermore, their use can help the reader of research to recognise the rationales behind the decisions that the investigator has made.

In designing a study the researcher may have to consider the concept of time and location. In this chapter various research designs, such as prospective (looking ahead), retrospective (looking backwards), *ex post facto* (after an event) and historical designs, will be discussed. As part of the prospective studies, cross-sectional and longitudinal research will also be examined.

Sometimes research studies are categorised according to their location. The terms 'field' and 'laboratory' studies are sometimes used and both have their advantages and disadvantages. Similarly, case studies may be conducted in a single centre, and phenomena examined from several positions using more than one research approach.

Before the researcher can begin the study, major decisions have to be made regarding the approach to be taken and the overall research design. The focus of the study may not be solely on the subject of the investigation but on the theory or the philosophical stance taken by the researcher.

The plethora of terms used to categorise different research studies will often confuse the newcomer to studying research. Quantitative research might be thought of as any type of research in which measurement is involved. The term 'quantitative' may refer to both the method of collecting the data and the type of data involved. The criteria revolve around whether or not the data are already in the numerical form or can be easily transformed into numbers.

At its basic form this numerical data will include the frequency in which a phenomenon occurs. At the more sophisticated end of the scale exact measurements will be recorded under very strict conditions. The importance of recognising the character-istics of these different levels of measurement is emphasised and discussed fully in Chapter 9. The data collection methods most frequently employed in quantitative research include the use of questionnaires and structured interviews.

In order to produce data collecting tools or instruments which will accurately measure the phenomena being studied, the researcher will need to have considerable knowledge of the subject/phenomena under scrutiny. A frequent criticism of quantitative data is that there is not enough evidence that the data collecting tool is actually measuring the phenomena under study.

Researchers may not collect their own data but use that already collected by another agency. National archives may hold data collected by various organisations, such as academic and government departments, to which researchers may have access. Gilbert (2001) suggests that this type of research is gaining popularity among social researchers as it offers those with limited resources an opportunity to study large-scale data sets. With most organisations now using computerised infor-mation systems of some kind the amount of data which potentially could be available for researchers is increasing all the time. In an effort to utilise the results from many small studies **meta-analysis** is also recognised as a legitimate way of re-analysing quantitative data to produce more meaningful results.

In contrast, qualitative research methods adopt a much more flexible approach to data collection. Observational studies in which behaviours are observed and fully recorded are rarely in numerical form. Similarly, focused interviews in which the researcher holds a 'conversation' with the subjects, produces data that are often described as 'rich' in detail.

Thus this one classification of research, qualitative and quan-titative, identifies a research approach and, possibly more relevant, a type of data collection and subsequent analysis. Although usually presented as fairly 'tight' compartments, studies may include different methods of data collection which encompass both categories. In some cases researchers purposely use more than one approach to investigate a phenomenon. The term **'triangulation'** may be used to describe studies which collect data in different ways (data triangulation) or use different researchers (researcher triangulation). In essence, the use of triangulation adds weight to the findings.

Inductive and deductive approaches to research

A further classification frequently seen in research texts is that of inductive and deductive (hypothetico-deductive) research. This classification may give a much wider understanding of the researcher's stance within the research study which goes beyond the method of data collection.

Miller (1985) cited by Bassett (1994) proposed that researchers needed to consider various ideas prior to commencing a study. These ideas include: the existing research-based knowledge of the topic being studied; the purpose of the research; whether the study is to discover information or to confirm existing knowledge; and the capability of the researcher to obtain the required data.

Possibly most important is the researcher's attitude to gaining knowledge. A major way in which new knowledge is gained is through logical reasoning and this falls into the two categories of inductive and deductive reasoning. As research is about the gaining of new knowledge it makes sense that types of research are often identified under the two headings of inductive theory development, and deductive theory testing.

It can be seen therefore that the terms 'inductive' and 'deductive' are related to the place of theory within the study. In simplistic terms, inductive research generates theories which are then tested through deductive research.

Polit and Beck (2006) suggest that inductive and hypothetico-deductive approaches to research should be called methodologies. They argue that such approaches are more than a way of collecting data; rather they are an overall commitment within the research process. From the literature it would appear that the other approaches to research such as phenomenology and feminism should also be referred to as methodologies as they identify a belief or position from which the researcher conducts the study. In more recent years the term 'emancipatory' research has been used to describe research methodologies which attempt to restore a balance between the researcher and the researched. Particularly in quantitative research there has been a quest for objective research to be carried out 'on' people.

The growing use of **action research** in which a problem is studied at a local level, with those being studied being equally involved in all decisions about the project has helped bridge the gap and speed up the **implementation** of any changes resulting from the research findings. However, as Karim (2001) identifies in his enlightening review on the strengths and weaknesses of action research, it is very time consuming and really best suited to small scale studies. In a more focused manner, **feminist research** has attempted to add the voice of women to studies of society in which they perceived their views had been previously hidden.

The approach and design of research selected should ultimately relate to the research question being posed (see Chapter 6). The design needs to enable the researcher to address the research question. A question asking about experiences of care received can be answered through a qualitative study using phenomenology, which might employ interview techniques to explore individual views of care.

Inductive approaches

Inductive reasoning moves from the general to the particular. In research it usually starts off with a set of observations of a situation. From this early stage the researcher would plan to document the information very carefully. This inductive approach in research encaptures the philosophy that people are fundamentally different from things, and should be valued as individuals. As patterns of behaviour or interactions develop the researcher seeks to make sense of them from the individual's perspective.

When undertaking inductive research there are several points that the researcher must be clear about regarding the approach to data collection. Initially, whatever data collection methods are used, a great effort must be made by the researcher not to influence the collection of data. This research approach demands that the picture painted is as close to the real situation as possible as there is no attempt at interpretation. In the account of the observations, the physical environment is often described as well as the speech and actions of individuals so that a complete picture is painted.

From these ideas it may be seen that in undertaking inductive research a researcher may have certain beliefs about the individual in society. Burns and Grove (2005) suggest that there is a need for 'methodological congruence' or a 'fit' between the research design and the researcher's philosophical orientation.

Under the umbrella of inductive research there are various designs which require further discussion.

Ethnography

This approach has its roots in social anthropology, when researchers lived among the group of individuals being studied. The term 'going native' has been coined from these early studies and the work of ethnographers such as Mead who, in the 1930s, lived among tribes in Papua New Guinea (Haralambos, Holborn and Heald, 2004). In more modern times 'going native' might refer to joining groups which are being studied, such as football supporters or a group of homeless individuals. Whatever group is being studied the crucial point is that of becoming an 'insider', and experiencing the group or organisation 'as one of them', and not as an 'outsider' looking in. Manias and Street (2001) describe the use of **ethnography** to examine nurse–nurse and nurse–doctor interactions in a critical care hospital setting. Six registered nurses formed the participant group, with data collection including **participant observation**, individual and focus group interviews and the completion of a professional journal of professional interactivity. Here the researchers were part of the critical care environment and members of the health care professions, having 'insider' roles which they felt supported the generation of valuable insights into professional relationships.

In order to be able to study a group in such depth, the researcher has to enter the study without preconceptions about the group or the questions to be asked. Through observations and in-depth questioning, the researcher looks for connections, patterns and themes that have meaning for the people within that culture. These themes might include shared belief systems, language, or role behaviours.

Phenomenology

Phenomenology has its roots in European philosophy, and is based on knowledge gained within the experiences of the individual and the individual's view of the world. In this approach the research question is explained through 'lived experiences' as described by those being studied. There is a basic belief by the researcher that individuals have attitudes, values and knowledge with which they make sense of their world and which guide their actions. Burns and Grove (2005) argue that phenomenologists view the individual as being integral with their environment and that every experience is unique. Therefore the role of phenomenology is to describe the experience being studied rather than attempt to define or explain it. Beauregard and Solomon (2005) used phenomenology in an attempt to examine the experiences of five women living with HIV/AIDS and to begin to explore the implications of these findings for occupational therapy. In the study there is an explanation of the interrelationship between exploring the lived experience and reflecting on the unique themes of the experience for the women and occupational therapists. In general the researcher strives to capture the richness of the experience while maintaining a strong orientation to the fundamental research question (van Manen, 1990).

Grounded theory

Grounded theory as an approach to research was developed by Glaser and Strauss (1967). They generated a systematic procedure for developing a theory about a phenomenon from the collected data. As the researcher examines the data, which have been collected by observations or interviews, themes and concepts are identified. The researcher then returns frequently to the data looking for further evidence of the themes, and revising the research question as issues arise from the data. A grounded theory approach was used by Price and Mitchell (2004) in their study of teenage women's experiences of the maternity services. It allowed the participants to articulate their own ideas about maternal care and permitted the researchers to be guided in their interviews by the data they were collecting.

To use grounded theory, the researcher needs to have knowledge of the literature and people's experience with the situation being examined. The literature is used to provide the researcher with prompts and guidance over the concepts related to the area under investigation. In many ways, grounded theory is perceived as the far end of the inductive continuum as theories are actually produced. In phenomenology and ethnography the themes and categories describing behaviours in their social context are often the end point of the study.

Evaluation research

Evaluative research focuses on collecting data to ascertain the effects of some form of planned change (Gilbert, 2001). Such research aims to find out whether a particular policy or intervention is working. It might be applied to look at the effects of a new policy initiative in the National Health Service (NHS), such as the effect of new roles in nursing, for example, the modern matron, or the impact of assistant practitioner roles in the allied health professions. In researching the effectiveness of new roles, the outcomes of the research would aim to help policy-makers in the NHS decide whether the new roles should be extended, changed or completely replaced. The research focus is therefore to evaluate the effects of change in practice brought about by new policy or initiatives, rather than to generate new knowledge. The research designs employed by researchers can include qualitative and quantitative methods.

Deductive approaches

Deductive reasoning moves from the specific to the general. In research terms this means a prediction is made of the presence or not, of a difference or a relationship between two or more factors (usually referred to as **variables**). The prediction is made through a hypothesis or measurable statement that can be deduced from a theory. This prediction will then be tested. The results of the research will either support the prediction or not, thereby confirming the theory or not.

In essence, deductive or hypothetico-deductive research depends on several considerations to withstand scrutiny. The first requirement is that there must be an existing theory on which to base the hypothesis, and give the study a focus. Following that, a previously tested data collecting tool will be needed to collect information from a **representative sample** of the research population. The analysis of the results will demand rigorous statistical testing in which the possibility of these results occurring by chance will be demonstrated and discussed. Deductive research tends to be tightly managed and highly structured, to allow the movement of the findings from the specific sample to a more general research population. This movement is sometimes referred to as the generalisability of the results.

Surveys

Surveys are widely used to collect information from a large number of people. They are primarily designed to study the relationship and incidence of variables in a population, such as attitudes and values and demographic details, for example, age and type of living accommodation. Questionnaires are frequently used to collect this information, with the respondent completing a self-administered form and returning it to the researcher. A telephone may also be used, and the respondents' replies noted immediately. Evans et al. (2005) provide an example of a telephone survey where mental health service managers were asked how approved social work status was felt to impact on work patterns and workload stress of staff. It allowed the researcher to 'interview' a large sample of individuals from a wide geographical area. However, there can be drawbacks. The researcher has to acknowledge that a number of people will just put the phone down, and those who have particular hearing difficulties may need to be excluded from the sample (as do those without a telephone). Furthermore, in surveys, face-to-face interviews can be used, where the researcher tends to obtain more information and a high rate of returns as few people refuse to be interviewed. However, it is a time-consuming procedure, and the sample would be much smaller than that used with a questionnaire.

There are two main types of surveys: descriptive and correlational. In descriptive surveys, data are collected from a sample of individuals and the results describe the situation as the researchers found it. For example, in a survey of social work students who qualified in 2005 the researcher might describe the number who now work in social services, those who work in the independent sector and those who do not practise. There is no further analysis beyond the description. A correlational survey goes further. In this type of survey the results include a description of the findings, but the researcher then seeks to find relationships between the characteristics (variables) in which they were interested, such as whether social workers have taken up posts with children and young people.

Experimental/quasi-experimental designs in research

The ability of the researcher to control or manipulate elements of the study renders experimental research different from other approaches (Cormack, 2000). In experimental research the researcher is interested in the effect of different treatments on two or more groups which have been matched. Usually this means manipulating the **independent variable** (or cause) and examining and measuring the **dependent variable** (or effect).

In true experimental research the investigator is an active agent who has responsibility in three specific areas:

1   Randomisation – subjects are assigned to the experimental or **control group** in a randomised manner. Everyone in the study must have an equal chance of being included in any group.
2   Control – there must be a control group who receive the traditional or usual care/treatment.
3   Manipulation – the researcher must have an **experimental group** receiving different care/treatment.

When these three conditions are stringently applied, the results of true **experiments** in examining a causal relationship are most powerful.

Although the results of experiments are powerful there are many problems using them. The ethical considerations associated with using human beings in experiments limits their use. Cormack (2000) also suggests that a problem with using experiments can be that of the 'Hawthorne' effect, in which people alter their behaviour when they know they are part of a study. When this happens the results of the experiment might be affected.

Because of these problems in conducting experiments the notion of **quasi-experiments** has been developed. There is still the manipulation of the independent variable, but there may be limited randomisation, or use of a control group. The results of quasi-experiments are therefore considerably weaker than those of true experiments. The term quasi-experiments is also used to describe experimental studies which lack one or more of the conditions noted above.

In the most controlled settings a laboratory may be used. It may not look like a traditional laboratory as, in some studies, buildings have been made to look like prisons or hospital wards in order to set up an experiment.

An alternative to a laboratory experiment is to use a field approach. In this type of experiment the research is conducted wherever the subjects are likely to be found, such as in a clinic, a hospital ward or in the street. Often field experiments are quasi-experiments, as it is often difficult to control all variables. Experiments which take place in practice settings involving patients/clients are commonly called randomised clinical trials (RCT). In a study to examine the effect of 'forcing' patients to use their affected arm following a stroke, van der Lee et al. (2000) randomly allocated a group of 66 patients with a chronic hemiplegia into either a 'control' group which had the traditional therapy, or an experimental group which had their unaffected arm immobilised so they were 'forced' to use their affected arm. After two weeks, all patients were assessed by an observer who was unaware of their grouping, who measured the mobility of their affected arm. The results identified a small improvement in the experimental treatment group. In this case the trial would be referred to as a 'single blind trial' as the observers were unaware of which group the patient was in, but clearly the patient and their carers knew the group. In trials where no one involved with the experiment knows which group the participants are in (for example, drug trials where placebos are used) the term 'double blind' is used.

Ex post facto research designs

Ex post facto literally means 'after the fact'. In these studies there is an investigation about a relationship between two or more variables, but after the events have been allowed to happen in the natural course of events. The two most common forms of *ex post facto* research designs are retrospective and prospective studies. In retrospective studies the researcher wants to study an effect, and will search for some causative factor of that effect. Prospective studies are conducted in the light of presumed causes. Researchers will follow their subjects forward in time and look for an effect which is due to the presumed cause. Prospective studies are usually expensive and time consuming due to the need to follow up subjects but they do allow the researcher a greater degree of control.

In the following section we shall look at some other research approaches.

Feminist research

From its beginnings as research conducted by feminists, feminist research has developed into a research methodology in its own right. Feminist research attempts to redress the balance of many years of male dominance in explanations of what happens in our society. It does this by developing a non-threatening, non-hierarchical relationship between the researcher and the subjects, and by making women the focus of the study. May (1997) argues that to gain a fuller understanding of our social life in general the role of gender must play a central part in any sociological investigation. To do anything else, it is suggested, would be a distortion of the social world. There is an argument regarding the position of men conducting feminist research. In principle some believe it possible (Harding, 1987, cited by Webb, 1993); others believe that men, by not encountering a woman's experience, are unable to conduct the research from a woman's position (Kremer, 1990, cited by Webb, 1993). In an attempt to recognise exactly what is feminist research, Cook and Fonow (1986) identified five characteristics:

1 The attention given to the significance of gender.
2 Consciousness raising (of women's issues).
3 A rejection of the concept of objectivity.
4 The recognition of the exploitation of women.
5 The empowerment of women as a result of the research.

As a methodology, feminist research is not constrained by a particular data-collecting method. However, the very nature of feminist research in which there is involvement of the researcher with the researched, and a sharing of experiences, would imply a need for a more open and **inductive** research approach rather than a closed deductive approach.

Action research

Action research is an approach which attempts to bring about a change in practice. This occurs through action, and reflection on that action, while developing an improvement in practice. Thus action research may be described as a spiral of self-reflection, in which individuals question the familiar and explore the unfamiliar (Stark, 1994). Alongside the change in practice is the development and testing of theories using hypotheses. According to Titchen and Binnie (1994) there are two main elements they call 'outsider' and 'insider' research. The insider refers to the professionals who are developing their practice while being involved in the research. The outsider is the researcher who observes the insider's practice, and provides an opportunity for the insider to rationalise and discuss the practice while examining the methodological considerations. This discussion has been taken further by Regehr (2000) who argues that action research is not simply about a form of research which gives equal status to researcher and professional, but also between researcher and the 'person in the street'. Action research was used to involve the staff and management of a homeless night shelter to institute tangible improvements in service delivery (Payne, 2002). The inclusion of staff and managers in the research aided the development of the service.

Action research attempts to influence the real world by identifying these changes as they take place rather than generating theories. However, there is an argument that action research should begin by observations, either completed in a prior study, or as a preliminary to the action research in which theories may have been generated.

Hanson and Clarke (2000) recognise that although action research has traditionally has been placed within a qualitative classification it actually spans a much wider base. They demonstrate the qualities of action research as a means of evaluating the introduction of new services to enhance the autonomy, independence and quality of life of frail older people in the community (Hanson and Clarke, 2000).

Case Studies

Case study research is growing in popularity, as it allows researchers to conduct small-scale studies around a specific situation. For example, in a study which investigated the care of patients with dementia in hospital, a specific patient might be the 'case' and the researcher would use qualitative and quantitative approaches to investigate all aspects of care, including the role of each member of the multi-disciplinary team, communication systems around the care delivered, the role of social workers in supporting the family etc. In another example, a school might be the 'case', and all aspects of the school would be investigated, perhaps examining why one school had a higher truancy rate than another. An in-depth discussion of the use of case studies may be found in Bergen and While (2000) and Gomm, Hammersley and Foster (2000).

Historical research

Historical research has the goal of attaining new knowledge from the systematic collection and critical evaluation of data that relate to past events. Polit and Beck (2006) suggest this research approach can rely primarily on qualitative data and examines causes, effects and trends of past events, considering how they might inform present behaviours and practices. Sources of data can include documents, records, eyewitness accounts and oral histories. Kirby (2004) used a historical approach to provide an understanding of the present range of views about the current position and future of nursing research. Documentary sources used included government reports and professional journals from the 1950s, 1960s and 1970s; these years are seen as the foundation periods for nursing research.

Systematic reviews

Increasingly, systematic reviews of previously published research are being written and used by health and social care workers. Crookes and Davies (1998) support the notion that a systematic review should identify all the research published on a given topic, and is completed by a synthesis of all the findings. As an exemplar of this process, the **Cochrane Library** databases can be accessed to inform the reader of the results of a systematic review of randomised controlled trials on various topics. However, there are also many examples of systematic reviews in the health and social care literature which take a much wider remit and consider both qualitative and quantitative studies. Many institutions of higher education also use **systematic literature reviews** as a basis for dissertation work. The required skills of critical appraisal and research synthesis are seen as important as collecting and analysing small data sets. An example of systematic review on the treatment for acute bronchiolitis for paediatric patients between 0–24 months old can be found in the work of Perrotta, Ortiz and Rogue (2005). In this review the researchers included papers from a number of databases. It was highlighted that chest physiotherapy using vibration and percussion techniques does not reduce the length of hospitalised stay or oxygen requirements.

Meta-analyses

Similar to systematic literature reviews are meta-analyses. However, in this case the actual findings of reviewed quantitative studies are amalgamated and reworked. This process can be helpful when there are many small studies on a topic, which on their own are too small to demonstrate an effect but which can produce substantial results when analysed together. Therefore, it can be possible to draw conclusions when looking at the data from a number of studies that may not have been possible from each individual study. They can also aid in gaining a consensus and agreement on best practice when there are inconsistencies in the results of published studies. Kent, Marks, Pearson and Keating (2005) compared the quantitative outcomes of ten randomised controlled trials to explore the effects of mobilisation and manipulation in the treatment of non-specific low back pain. They looked at research where the clinician was either able or unable to select a specific treatment. The findings of the meta-analysis suggested that the ability to tailor manual therapy treatment to the individual was not likely to have a positive impact on patient outcomes. Polit and Beck (2006) provide further explanations of this research approach.

Mixed-methods

The objective of **mixed-methods** studies is to use different data collection methods to address research questions, gaining different perspectives from the data and giving a fuller view and broader research understandings. Mixed-methods research may triangulate methods of data collection, using three or more methods of collecting data (see Chapter 8). It is preferable that the methods used are drawn from both qualitative and quantitative traditions. Given the scope of mixed-methods research its use is increasing in health and social care studies. Nicolson, Burr and Powell (2005) report the use of mixed-methods to ascertain the educational and working experiences of advanced practitioners in neonatal nursing and identify subsequent training needs of the graduates. The research employed interviews, focus groups and a survey, providing both qualitative and quantitative data.

Key Points

- The place of theory within research is important.
- Inductive research attempts to develop a theory.
- Deductive research tests theories.
- Both these categories have further sub-divisions.
- Action research attempts to change practice while the research is ongoing.
- Feminist research has a particular approach, and is not tied to a specific data collecting method.
- Research can employ mixed-methods.

Further Reading

Gilbert, N. (2001). *Researching social life* (2nd ed.). London: Sage.

Gomm, R., Hammersley, M. and Foster, P. (Eds.) (2000). *Case study method.* London: Sage.

Hicks, C. (2004). *Research methods for clinical therapists: applied project design and analysis* (4th ed.). London: Churchill Livingstone.

Hughes, C. (2002). *Key concepts in feminist theory and research.* London: Sage.

McNiff, J. (2003). *You and your action research project.* London: Routledge Falmer.

Polit, D. and Beck, C. (2006). *Essentials of nursing research: methods, appraisal and utilization* (6th ed.). Philadelphia: Lippincott Williams and Wilkins.

Stem, E. (2005). *Evaluation research methods.* London: Sage.

Thyer, B. (2001). *The handbook of social work research methods.* Thousand Oaks: Sage.

Wilkinson, G. (2005). Illustrating triangulation in mixed-methods research. *Nurse Researcher, 12* (4), 7–18.

6 Research Problems, Aims, Questions and Hypotheses

Learning Outcomes

On completion of this chapter the reader should be able to:

- appreciate the nature of research problems
- understand the formation of research questions
- recognise the difference between research questions and hypotheses
- identify independent and dependent variables.

Key Terms

- dependent variable
- hypothesis
- independent variable
- null hypotheses
- research problem
- research question

Introduction

The health and social care professions demand that practice should influence the identification of problems and questions that are researchable. These 'problems' may have their foundation in the experience and professional practice of individuals, or they may emerge from an existing theory. Researchable problems could also come from the results of previous published research that has identified some new problems or areas that need further research.

In many instances, a problem in practice is identified locally by a health and social care practitioner who feels that something is 'not quite right'. However, they may not feel in any position to do something about the problem. Occasionally this may lead directly to a research project being undertaken. More commonly, health and social care practitioners will be required to review all previously published research and critically appraise it. This will enable the practitioner to look at the problem and consider ways to overcome it.

Other chapters have considered the skills needed by health and social care practitioners to retrieve and critically appraise research findings and literature, and Chapter 3 deliberates upon the research process. This chapter examines research questions, aims and hypotheses, and takes up the position that nursing research questions often arise from problems in practice.

Research problems

Health and social care practitioners need to understand and identify research problems, which can then form the basis of a researchable question. They may not necessarily be involved in undertaking the research. However, they have an important role in identifying researchable questions and setting the agenda for research in practice.

Research problems may also be generated by large organisations that, in turn, identify priorities for research. The National Institute for Health and Clinical Excellence (NICE), for example, produces clinical guidelines and having already reviewed all the available evidence will then say where there is a gap in the evidence and a need for further research in specific areas. For some organisations, such as the Department of Health, research priorities will be identified and funding awarded for appropriate studies that address the problems.

At an early stage in the research process, a researcher needs to refine the problem into a clear researchable question(s). The way in which a research question is interpreted, however, is dependent on the beliefs, values, experience and approach of the researcher. When reading research, all health and social care practitioners should be aware of the researcher's influence in the way that research questions have been developed from the research problem.

As identified in Chapter 5, there are two broad approaches in research – deductive (often called quantitative research) and inductive (often called qualitative research). A deductive approach will use primarily quantitative methods of data collection and analysis to test a theory. On the basis of a theory, and prior to data collection, researchers will make predictions about what will happen in specific situations. An inductive approach, however, will use mainly qualitative methods of data collection and analysis with the aim of examining the data for patterns and relationships. The purpose is to understand and describe what is going on, with a view to generating a theory. Predictions may be generated from the data and tested and re-tested during the course of the research. However, research using this approach will not usually begin with a prediction about what will be found.

Research aims and objectives

Many researchers will identify aims and objectives at the beginning of their study. These will guide the researcher and give some indication of what the researcher is trying to achieve. Aims and objectives are not particularly specific; indeed, they may be intentionally vague. They may identify the purpose of the research, and they may suggest goals or outcomes in quite general terms. However, they do not give a clear indication of what questions are being asked, and they do not give any prediction as to what they are expecting to find. Both qualitative and quantitative studies may incorporate research aims and objectives.

Research questions

In order to be able to manage a research project the details of the study need to be made much more explicit, and this is often made clear through the research question(s). Some studies will have more than one research question, or there may be a principal question, followed by a few questions that are more specific. If there is more than one question, they must be clearly related. Most research will have research question(s) posed at the outset of the study, and qualitative studies using an inductive approach will continue to be guided by the questions. Exploratory studies, in particular, will identify research questions, occasionally with a view to generating and testing a theory from the descriptive findings of the study.

Clearly articulating and defining the research question is often identified as one of the most difficult stages in the research process. Cormack and Benton (Cormack, 2000: 78) suggest 'that a relationship between 2 or more variables is implied in a good research question'. The variables stated must be capable of observation and measurement. A research question can either be a statement in question form, or a statement of purpose: 'What is the relationship between the provision of post-registration education and the retention of staff?', or 'The purpose of this study is to investigate the relationship between the provision of post-registration education and the retention of staff.'

When reading research reports, health and social care practitioners need to be able to identify the source of the research question(s), and how it has been developed from the problem. In some reports, only the problem is identified through a problem statement. If this is the case, the problem needs to clearly identify and define the research variables and the nature of the population being studied. In other types of research, neither the problem nor the research question will be identified. However, there should be a specific purpose to the study which identifies why the study is being conducted.

Research hypotheses

In some approaches to research, a hypothesis is devised before the study begins and will guide the whole study. The hypothesis goes further than a research question and is directly related to the research problem. It is used primarily, although not exclusively, in quantitative studies using a deductive approach. The hypothesis is a statement about the relationship between two or more variables and predicts an expected outcome. Variables are any characteristics about a person that can vary: age, sex, height, eye colour, etc. In some studies, the variables need to be clearly defined because they are not always obvious. The hypothesis will also determine who and what is to be studied, and the way that the findings are interpreted. Unlike a research question, a hypothesis will predict what will happen in a particular study and it can be a very powerful and persuasive tool.

At the end of a study, a research question never permits the investigator to say more than: 'This is how the world looked when I observed it.' In contrast, hypotheses permit the investigator to say: 'Based on my particular explanation about how the world works, this is what I expected to observe, and behold – that is exactly how it looked! For that reason my explanation of how the world works must be given credibility.' When a hypothesis is confirmed, the investigator is empowered to make arguments about knowledge that go far beyond what is available when a question has been asked and answered.

A hypothesis can also be stated as a **'null' hypothesis**. The null hypothesis states that there is *no* relationship between the variables. The null hypothesis is the preferred approach in some quantitative studies and is associated with tests of **statistical significance**. Hypotheses and null hypotheses are never 'proved' or 'disproved' in the truest sense of the word. They are accepted or rejected.

A hypothesis should be clear, concise, logical and specific enough for a reader to understand what the variables are and whom the researcher will be studying. A hypothesis will predict a relationship between variables (for example, difference, greater than, less than, positively, negatively) and, through testing, may or may not allow the relationship to be supported. There are two types of variable – independent variables and dependent variables. The independent variable is the 'treatment' or 'intervention' variable in the predicted relationship stated in the hypothesis; and the dependent variable is the 'outcome' variable in the relationship. This is commonly known as the 'cause and effect' relationship. There are some examples in Table 6.1.

All health and social care practitioners need to be able to recognise research aims, questions and hypotheses when they are reading research reports. The research questions or hypotheses identified should be clearly linked with the original research problem. Not all studies will have a hypothesis. However, where there is one, it should be clearly stated with at least two variables.

Table 6.1 *Independent and dependent variables within hypotheses*

Older nurses are less likely to express positive comments about the extended role of the nurse than younger nurses.

- Age of nurse is the independent variable.
- Positive comments about the extended role of the nurse is the dependent variable.

Patients who receive a copy of a leaflet about their condition will ask more questions about their care than those who do not receive a leaflet.

- Receiving/not receiving the NHS plan is the independent variable.
- Number of questions asked is the dependent variable.

Absenteeism is higher in social work students than radiography students.

- Type of student is the independent variable.
- Number of days absent is the dependent variable.

Elderly patients in residential care who experience back massage express greater satisfaction of care than those who do not receive back massage.

- Back massage is the independent variable.
- Satisfaction with care is the dependent variable.

Key Points

- Researchable problems have their foundations in practice, literature or an existing theory.
- An early stage in the research process is the identification of research aims, questions and hypotheses which must relate to the problem.
- A hypothesis is a statement about a relationship between two or more variables and predicts an expected outcome.

Further Reading

Blaxter, L. Hughes, C. and Tight, M. (1996). *How to research.* Buckingham: Open University Press.

Booth, A. (2001). Turning research priorities into answerable research questions. *Health Information and Libraries Journal, 18* (2), 130–132.

Cormack, D. and Benton, D. (2000). Asking the research question. In D. Cormack (Ed.). *The research process in nursing* (4th ed.) (pp. 77–88). Oxford: Blackwell Science.

LoBiondo-Wood, G. and Haber, J. (Eds.) (1998). *Nursing research: methods, critical appraisal, and utilization* (4th ed.). St. Louis, MO: Mosby.

National Institute for Health and Clinical Excellence: www.nice.org.uk

National Service Frameworks: check websites relevant to topic area, e.g.: mental health, coronary heart disease, diabetes.

Polit, D., Beck C. and Hungler, B. (2001). *Nursing research: principles and methods* (5th ed.). Philadelphia: J. B. Lippincott Co.

Robson, C. (2002). *Real world research*. Oxford: Blackwell Publishers.

Social Care Institute of Excellence: www.scie.org.uk

7 Sampling

Learning Outcomes

On completion of this chapter the reader should be able to:

- understand definitions of research populations and samples
- identify different sampling strategies that can be employed to select probability and non-probability samples
- consider issues surrounding gaining access to participants
- appreciate the factors that affect sample selection, including sampling criteria and sample size.

Key Terms

- non-probability sample ■ convenience/accidental sample
- purposive sample ■ representative sample ■ sampling
- stratified sample ■ target population ■ generalisation
- systematic sample ■ cluster sample ■ probability sample
- simple random sample ■ sample ■ selection criteria
- snowball sample ■ quota sample ■ bias

Introduction

Sampling is used in everyday life: for example, when we taste a sip of wine before deciding to buy a bottle or case of it, or at the supermarket we might handle and smell fruit before purchase. Sampling involves the collection of information on which decisions can be based and conclusions drawn. For example, if we liked the taste of the sampled wine we expect to get the same pleasure from bottles containing the same vintage, but could not be certain of our reactions if we purchased a vintage that we had not sampled.

Researchers must collect information from chosen samples, which is then used to make decisions and draw conclusions, just as the purchaser of wine does. The selection of the sample is therefore a very important part of the research process. The researcher needs to be confident in drawing conclusions based on the information collected from the chosen sample. Errors in sampling have the potential to invalidate the research findings and render the research unusable.

Before a sample is selected the researcher identifies a target population, using techniques which fall into two main sampling strategies, probability and non-probability sampling. Prior to describing these strategies, the terms 'target population' and 'sample' must be understood.

Target population

The target population includes the entire membership of the group in which the researcher is interested and from which information can be collected. Such populations might include all students following an undergraduate social work course, all National Health Service (NHS) Trust Hospitals, all physiotherapists. Researchers may also collect information from care/clinical situations or documents and in these cases the target population may include all cardio-pulmonary resuscitation attempts, or all completed care-planning documents.

The researcher can assign eligibility criteria to the target population, defining limits within which the target population must fall. For example, the researcher may be interested in the students following a course in therapeutic radiography rather than those following a course in diagnostic radiography. It is therefore necessary to define the target population as students following a course in therapeutic radiography and then select a sample of students who meet this criterion.

The definition of criteria by the researcher facilitates the generalisation (application) of the research findings. In the example given above, research findings could only reliably be applied to students following a course in therapeutic radiography. The degree to which results can be generalised is referred to as external validity. External validity can be an important factor in research. However, it should be acknowledged that not all researchers are interested in achieving **external validity**. Researchers using an inductive (qualitative) approach (see Chapter 5) will value the quality of the information collected rather than the ability to generalise the findings to a larger population.

Sampling

It is unlikely that the researcher will be able to collect information from the entire target population. This would be both time consuming and expensive. The researcher collects information from a representative sample of the target population, selected by taking a sample from the target population.

A sample is a portion, or part of, the target population, and is composed of members (elements or subjects) from which information is collected. In health and social care research the target population may be a patient or client group and the sample will be a portion of that patient or client group.

The most important feature of sampling is the degree to which the sample represents the target population. For the sample to be representative, the members need to reflect the target population in as many ways as possible. For example, how closely do the characteristics or variables such as gender, age, social care needs, medical diagnosis of the sample, reflect those of the target population?

The reduction of **sampling bias** is also of importance and can be seen if one part of the target population is over-represented or under-represented in the sample. For example, if the researcher was interested in measuring the effectiveness of health promotion strategies and chose to sample people attending health promotion clinics, it might be argued that those attending the clinics could have strong views about the benefits of the clinics, so may be a biased sample.

Limiting the difference between the target population and the sample is achieved to varying degrees through the application of accepted sampling techniques in the selection of samples. The two strategies used to select a sample are probability and non-probability sampling.

Probability samples

Probability sampling involves the use of random selection in obtaining the sample members. The use of random selection allows the researcher to state the **probability** of a member of the target population appearing in the sample. In some cases all members of the target population may have an equal chance of appearing in the sample. Probability sampling limits **sampling errors** and bias, increases sample representativeness and gives confidence in the sample. It is therefore the preferred sampling strategy when the researcher is interested in obtaining a representative sample.

Quantitative research designs often employ large probability samples in conducting surveys, experimental and quasi-experimental research (see Chapter 5). It should be noted, however, that qualitative researchers may also use random sampling techniques.

Simple random sample

In generating a simple random sample the basic technique of probability sampling is used. When the entire population is known, the use of simple random sampling gives each member of the target population an equal chance of being included in the sample. This occurs through the design of a **sampling frame** in which all members of the target population are represented and from which the sample will be chosen.

The researcher can generate the sampling frame, or an existing sampling frame may be used. If a researcher was interested in sampling qualified and practising nurses and midwives then the register held by the Nursing and Midwifery Council could be accessed and used as a sampling frame.

The use of existing sampling frames can be effective in accessing a sample but a sampling frame needs to be selected appropriately to avoid introducing sampling bias. For example, many market researchers use the telephone directory as a sampling frame. However, it should be acknowledged that as a sampling frame the telephone directory will be an incomplete list of the residents of a community. Not every resident will have a telephone and some of those with a telephone could be ex-directory. The telephone directory will not offer a complete

Table 7.1 *Random number table*

03	35	11	98	74	20	23	61	32	30
07	09	15	22	21	88	94	90	50	71
84	10	02	91	24	35	47	63	99	04
13	82	31	44	70	65	38	80	92	01
23	33	18	76	97	06	64	53	70	98
17	21	09	05	14	30	31	82	54	56
77	62	02	19	27	48	59	92	71	25
66	04	12	55	42	60	83	24	37	22
05	90	08	69	33	93	57	74	29	10
30	44	74	28	09	67	24	18	99	81
45	89	12	75	65	22	48	21	08	55
78	26	72	03	28	91	36	42	10	89
88	56	23	14	73	54	22	07	52	39
25	78	65	91	63	45	71	01	86	49
67	04	30	05	73	29	96	39	24	49
14	71	27	18	46	28	34	97	24	12
16	48	73	92	45	29	37	19	28	10
13	85	49	37	40	16	72	95	41	08
17	39	73	37	19	91	65	28	76	95
45	42	97	28	02	36	73	95	46	99
77	54	28	16	34	07	16	94	73	54
65	48	27	04	62	48	37	19	21	45
24	91	54	38	18	35	42	87	06	72
06	12	21	26	29	44	79	13	19	46
12	05	43	05	51	10	78	36	58	25
18	25	37	19	54	28	75	53	24	82
96	14	52	75	62	01	99	53	24	42
45	68	24	02	15	73	57	28	27	25
56	81	72	24	04	38	26	78	15	29

sampling frame and will not therefore facilitate probability sampling. There are a number of approaches that can be used to achieve randomisation with the website www.randomization.com proving a useful resource.

Having generated or obtained an existing sampling frame, the researcher proceeds to randomly select sufficient members from the frame to meet the sample size needed for the study. This can be achieved through the use of a random number table (see Table 7.1) or more inventive methods such as selecting names from a hat or using a blindfold and a pin. The use of the random number table necessitates numbering the sampling frame members and then selecting from the sampling frame, the numbers which correspond with those on the random number table. If selecting a sample of 10 from the random number table of a population of 100 in Table 7.1, the following numbered members would be included in the sample: 03, 35, 11, 98, 74, 20, 23, 61, 32, 30.

Halford, Price, Kelly, Bouma and Young (2005) employed random number tables to allocate participants to one of three treatment groups as part of a randomised controlled trial (see Chapter 5). The research assessed the effectiveness of three approaches to assisting 61 female partners of male problem drinkers cope with stress imposed by the male's drinking. The use of the random number table facilitated the allocation of the females to one of the three study groups; they would receive supportive counselling, or stress management, or alcohol-focused couples therapy. All three treatments led to a reduction in the women's reported stress.

In selecting a sample through simple random selection, it is apparent that the researcher cannot intentionally introduce sampling bias. Any bias, which may occur, will do so by accident, as a result of chance. The likelihood of introducing bias by chance will reduce as the size of the sample selected increases.

It is also apparent that the use of simple random sampling is laborious, and, despite the availability of computer software to generate random numbers, is time consuming. Simple random sampling can be used infrequently in sample selection, though the technique of random selection is seen in other probability sampling strategies.

Systematic random sample

In selecting a systematic random sample a similar technique to that of simple random sampling is employed, as a list of the target population is used to form a sampling frame from which the sample is selected on a systematic basis. In selecting systematically, the researcher may choose for example, every tenth member on the list or every hundredth member. In this way all members have an equal chance of being selected into the population, provided that all members of the target population are included in the sampling frame and that the sample is not already listed in some sort of systematic way, such as sister grade of nurse through to health care assistant.

It is possible to select the sample by first calculating the sampling interval for a target population (interval needed between each target member to be selected). To calculate the sampling interval, the researcher would need to know the total number in the target population and the sample size required. For example, if the total target population were 2000 women who attended an antenatal clinic, and the sample size required were 100 (2000/100 = 20), then the sample interval is 20. The researcher would select every twentieth woman, following on from the first woman selected from the sampling frame. If the first woman selected was identified as number 2, then women 22, 42, 62, 82, 102 etc. would form the sample.

This sampling technique was applied by Hsu (2005) to select households to take part in research that examined Taiwan consumers' preferences and information needs and the problems they encountered when getting information from medical websites. The sample included 10,432 residents of Taipei. Possible participants were identified from 28 boroughs, with 1 in every 60 households being selected to form the final sample.

Systematic sampling offers a more efficient way of selecting a random sample and the only way that bias can be introduced is by chance. For example, if every sixtieth participant selected by Hsu (2005) possessed a particular characteristic, that characteristic would be over-represented in the sample. In this example, every sixtieth participant may have been a single person household or member of the medical profession. A sample such composed could be argued to be biased and interpretation of the research findings would need to acknowledge this. As with simple random sampling, the chance of bias would be reduced as the size of the sample increased.

Stratified random sample

Selecting a stratified random sample involves the sub-division of the target population into strata, before developing a sampling frame from which a random sample is selected. It is dependent upon the researcher having knowledge of the characteristics or variables of the population, which are important to achieving a representative sample. Sub-division could relate to any variable or characteristic of the target population, such as age, sex, height, weight, ethnic group, socio-economic status, delivery of specific social care, diagnosis, period of admission to hospital or drug prescriptions.

Selecting a sample in this way can help achieve a representative sample with a smaller sample size, and so can facilitate more effective use of resources, especially time and money. For example, if a researcher were collecting opinions from physiotherapists about sexual harassment at work, it would be important for the sample to represent the percentage of male and female physiotherapists in the workforce. If the proportion of males were 30% and females were 70%, then a proportionate sample would reflect this.

In some instances the researcher may feel it important to have equal numbers of respondents in the sample to obtain a more balanced view, in this case 50% male and 50% female. This would be a disproportionate sample as it does not represent the male and female composition of the physiotherapist group. The researcher would need to adjust the analysis of any results to compensate for this, by weighting responses. Explanation of this procedure is beyond the scope of this introductory text, but can be found in Kidder and Judd (1987), cited as further reading below.

Mizrahi and Berger's (2001) administrators used a stratified random sample to examine the responses of social work sampling to the changes occurring throughout their hospitals' major accomplishments, failures and barriers to the delivery of social work services. The researchers employed an exploratory-descriptive survey (see Chapter 5). Using the American Hospital Association membership list of 3700 hospitals, a stratified random sample of 750 were selected. The sample was stratified according to geographical location, bed size and stage of managed care development.

Stratified sampling enables the researcher to use a smaller sample size to obtain the same measure of representation achieved from a larger simple random sample. It is, therefore, more time and cost effective for the researcher, as using a smaller sample size reduces time spent on data collection and analysis. Sampling error is decreased as variables within the target population, which are critical to the research, are represented through stratification. To achieve this, the researcher has to have knowledge of the target population and, therefore, more effort is required in selecting a sample this way.

Cluster sample

Selecting a cluster sample is a more efficient way of accessing a larger sample than through simple or stratified sampling, and is often used to select samples for large-scale surveys, particularly in large geographical areas. Cluster samples can be obtained in situations where a sampling frame cannot be developed using individual members of the target population, as members are not all known to the researcher. This may occur if, for example, the target population were all patients having recovered from gynaecological surgery.

Cluster sampling can also be referred to as multi-stage sampling, as the researcher selects the sample by following through a number of stages. For example, if the researcher wanted to access patients following gynaecological surgery, a sampling frame composed of organisations treating gynaecological surgical patients would be developed and used to randomly select patients as sample members. The sampling frame may include: regional health authorities, trusts, units, wards and finally patients admitted to the wards. The researcher would firstly select a regional health authority and then randomly select trusts within that regional health authority. Surgical/gynaecological units would then be selected from the hospitals and gynaecological wards within those units would form the penultimate sample, with patients on the wards being the final sampling frame.

Cluster sampling is more prone to sampling error than simple, stratified and systematic sampling, but offers the researcher a more efficient way of sampling when a large-scale survey is required. As shown in the example, the technique can also be valuable to the researcher who does not have a sampling frame composed of individual target population members, but is able to commence the sampling process with a sampling frame of organisations or institutions. By following multi-stage sampling techniques, the required sample will be accessed.

Non-probability samples

Non-probability sampling techniques do not use random selection to gather together the sample. Researchers using non-probability sampling will not be able to state the probability of target population members being selected in the sample, as not every member of the target population has a chance of being selected in the sample. Non-probability sampling is more convenient to use, cost effective and can be used to select a research sample when the researcher does not know the membership of the target population. Non-probability sampling techniques include: convenience (accidental) sampling, quota sampling, purposive (judgemental) sampling and snowball sampling. These techniques are often employed in qualitative research designs such as ethnographic, phenomenological, grounded theory, exploratory and evaluative designs (see Chapter 5). This said, convenience sampling is commonly used and can be employed in quantitative studies as part of survey or quasi-experimental designs.

Convenience (accidental) sampling

When employing convenience or accidental sampling techniques the researcher obtains sufficient participants from the local or convenient target population. Participants are included in the sample because they are accessible. For example, a researcher considering the management of social care delivery may select a local sample rather than travelling some distance to obtain a sample.

This is an uncomplicated approach to sampling, which is time and cost effective. Consequently, convenience sampling is a commonly used method. Moule (2005) presents research that used such techniques. Drawing on a local sample of nursing, radiography and radiotherapy students from a conveniently located university, the research used a case study approach (see Yin, 1994) to consider whether students working online could develop as a learning community.

When employing convenience sampling techniques, it is important for the researcher to acknowledge any limitations in the sample. Convenience sampling is the weakest sampling technique because bias may be introduced into the sample; this is difficult to identify and therefore any effect on the results can be difficult to judge. Bias can result from the over-representation or under-representation of portions of the target population, or from the effect of the researcher sampling locally from a population that is known. Bias may also result if the participants self-select themselves into the sample, through perhaps responding to market researchers in the street or to advertisements for research participants.

Quota sampling

Selecting a quota sample involves the application of principles, which are similar to those used to select a stratified random sample. The researcher uses knowledge of the target population to ensure that certain variables or characteristics of the target population are represented in the sample. The researcher may wish to include any number of variables in the sample: for example, to represent males and females, socio-economic groups, individuals with certain health and social care needs, presence of disease or certain behaviour. By ensuring certain variables are represented in the sample, quota sampling offers a more reliable sampling technique than convenience sampling as it attempts to limit some potential biases.

Hung (2005) used a quota sample when conducting research (which aimed to revalidate the Hung Postpartum Stress Scale) to measure women's specific childbearing stressors during the postpartum period following childbirth. The sample was recruited from hospitals and clinics in Taiwan that had birth rates of 30 or more births per month. Those women included in the sample had to meet a number of inclusion criteria. They needed to be low-risk postpartum women who had delivered a single, healthy, full-term child without complications and had no postnatal complications or underlying medical problems. A quota was applied in the sampling strategy as the total number of women included from each hospital or clinic was proportionate to the total number of births. Thus, the hospital or clinic with the highest number of births had the highest number of women included in the final sample.

Purposive (judgemental) sampling

A purposive sample is selected using the researcher's judgement, with no external objective method being used in sample selection. Reliance on the researcher could be inappropriate and lead to the selection of a biased sample. For example, the researcher may choose sample members who will, it is felt, reflect a certain viewpoint.

Purposive sampling can be a useful sampling technique to employ when the researcher wants to obtain a particular sample which cannot easily be selected through any other technique. This approach to sampling was employed by Kealey and

McIntyre (2005) when evaluating a domiciliary occupational therapy service provided for patients in the palliative stage of cancer care. A purposive sample of 30 patients and their primary informal carers were selected to take part in structured interviewing. These participants were selected as users of the domiciliary service being evaluated.

Snowball sampling

A snowball sample can be a useful technique for selecting a 'hidden' sample group, such as the homeless. Snowball sampling is based on the assumption that people with like characteristics, behaviours or interests, form associations, and it is this relationship which the researcher uses to select a sample. For example, access to a group of experts can be gained by approaching one expert who recommends possible further respondents. Access to the homeless, drug abusers, alcoholics, can be obtained through one group member, who recommends further sample members and thus a self-generating sample is facilitated. Biases can be introduced as the sample is not independently selected and the sample could perpetuate particular traits. However, it can be a useful way of selecting a sample from marginalised groups.

Hughes, Sinha, Higginson, Down and Leigh (2005), who used the snowballing technique to sample people living with motor neurone disease, employed this approach. This qualitative research used semi-structured interviews to explore people's experiences of living with the disease, and invited those interviewed to pass on introductory letters to family and professionals, asking them to take part in the research.

Issues relating to sample size

There are no hard and fast rules governing the selection of sample size. The choice of the sample, using the techniques described in the chapter, is of greater importance than the choice of a particular sample size. However, a technique known as power analysis can be applied to estimate an appropriate sample size. This can be particularly applied in quantitative studies, when particular statistical tests are applied to the results and when the generalisation of results to a wider population is of importance. The discussion of power analysis is beyond the scope of this introductory text, but can be found in Burns and Grove (2005), included as further reading below.

It is generally accepted that a larger probability sample will give greater accuracy to the results, as the effect of over-representation or under-representation is reduced as the sample size increases. Non-probability samples may use a smaller sample size more effectively, particularly if the researcher is interested in the value of the quality of the information collected (qualitative approach), rather than the quantity of information which could be gathered (quantitative approach). Whichever sampling technique is used, it is the representative nature of the sample that is of greater importance than the size.

Gaining access to subjects

In order to undertake research it is necessary to gain access to the sources of data. In health and social care research these are generally people, but could also be records, documents or personally related data. Sometimes the sources of the data will be 'protected' and the researcher may need to negotiate carefully with people in powerful positions, or with institutions. The term '**gate-keeper**' is often used to describe people who are attempting to safeguard the interests of others. These could, for example, be teachers protecting students on a course, or managers protecting employees. When research is taking place in health or social care settings, such as clinics or wards, the researcher will need to gain permission from key individuals such as clinical managers. If patients, and in many cases staff, are involved, the proposed research will need to meet **research governance** requirements and be considered by a local Research Ethics Committee (see Chapter 10).

Acquiring permission or consent of the subjects is also an important factor in gaining access. This can be particularly difficult when the research is covert, such as participant observational studies.

Many ethical issues will need to be considered by the researcher, such as deception, concealment and not gaining consent from subjects who will clearly need to be protected. Dealing with gatekeepers and negotiating access is a responsibility that the researchers must take seriously in order to protect research integrity. When reading research critically, health and social care professionals must consider ways that the researcher may have negotiated this process.

Key Points

- Researchers must collect information from chosen samples.
- The researcher selects a sample from the target population.
- Sampling bias can occur if one element of the target population is over or under-represented.
- The two overall strategies used to select a sample, are probability and non-probability sampling.
- There are no hard and fast rules about the size of sample needed to support research, though the use of statistical tests in quantitative studies may dictate sample size.

Further Reading

Alston, M. and Bowles, W. (2003). *Research for social workers: an introduction to methods* (2nd ed.). London: Routledge.

Burns, N. and Grove, S. (2005). *The practice of nursing research: conduct, critique and utilization* (5th ed.). Philadelphia: Elsevier Saunders.

Burns, R.B. (2000). *Introduction to research methods*. London: Sage.

Department of Health (2005). *Research governance framework for health and social care* (2nd ed.). Available online: http://www.dh.gov.uk/publications/ (accessed 11.10.05).

Hicks, C. (1999). *Research methods for clinical therapists* (3rd ed.). Edinburgh: Churchill Livingstone.

Kidder, L. and Judd, C. (1987). *Research methods in social relations* (5th ed.). New York: CBS Publishing.

Polit, D. and Beck, C. (2006). *Essentials of nursing research: methods, appraisal and utilization* (6th ed.). Philadelphia: Lippincott Williams and Wilkins.

8 Understanding Data Collection Techniques

Learning Outcomes

On completion of this chapter the reader should be able to:

- appreciate the need for reliable and valid data collection methods in health and social care research
- identify the main data collection techniques used in health and social care research
- understand the need to choose data collection techniques appropriate to the research approach and design
- evaluate the advantages and disadvantages of different measuring instruments.

Key Terms

- documentary evidence ■ interview ■ Likert scale
- non-participant observer ■ rigour ■ secondary data collection ■ observation schedule ■ participant observer
- psychological measures ■ repertory grid ■ physiological measures ■ questionnaire ■ rating scale ■ reliability
- observation ■ trustworthiness ■ validity ■ Visual Analogue Scale ■ vignettes ■ triangulation

Introduction

Research information can be collected in many ways. The researcher's choice of data collection instrument is influenced by the research approach (qualitative or quantitative) and the research questions to be addressed. The researcher must be confident that the instrument or instruments used will collect information relevant to the research question, and support the research approach taken.

Reliability and validity

The researcher is also concerned about the reliability and validity of the data collection method used. Both reliability and validity are important as they afford credibility to the data collection tool and subsequent research findings. Polit and Beck (2006) suggest a valid and reliable instrument will measure what it is expected to measure, and be consistent or dependable in measuring what it is designed to measure. A valid instrument will therefore measure what it is supposed to measure, and a reliable instrument will always measure what it is supposed to measure. For example, the tympanic thermometer is seen as a valid and reliable way of measuring temperature. Unless broken it will measure a patient's temperature when the principles of correct temperature taking are followed, and will measure every patient's temperature in the same way.

It should be remembered that there is always room for error in measurement. For example, if the principles of correct temperature taking using a tympanic thermometer are not followed the thermometer may record an abnormally high or low temperature that would not reflect the patient's true temperature. Data collection is therefore open to some inconsistency. Any inconsistency should be acknowledged by the researcher and may lead to the adoption of research practices that will enhance reliability, such as using several data collection methods. If a data collection instrument is not, however, a valid measure, and is not recording what it is expected to, then the researcher must look to alternative measuring tools.

Establishing trustworthiness

Qualitative research methods are essentially different to quantitative methods and there is a need to evaluate qualitative methods against different and appropriate criteria. Lincoln and Guba (1985) present specific steps that can be taken to try to ensure rigour and **trustworthiness** in qualitative research: credibility, transferability, dependability and confirmability. To establish trustworthiness data must be auditable through checking that the interpretations are credible. The credibility of data is improved through long engagement with the respondents or triangulation (using three or more methods) of data collection. 'Thick' description of the research process can enable the reader to determine how transferable the results may be to another setting. An audit trail of the research assists in establishing the dependability of the research and confirmability, through the inclusion of information that might include the presentation of raw data and an explanation of data analysis processes. Mavundla (2000) provides a useful summary of the processes undertaken to ensure trustworthiness within qualitative research that explored professional nurses' perceptions of nursing mentally ill clients in general hospital settings. Mavundla (2000) discusses the use of prolonged engagement of three years in the field, triangulation of methods, and member checking (asking participants to verify analysis to support credibility). Transferability is supported by the provision of thick description of the methods used, and the engagement of an independent expert to code data and discuss this coding with the researcher supported dependability. Confirmability was afforded through the use of independent expert researchers who audited the project.

The most commonly used data collection instruments will be discussed in this chapter. These include: physiological and psychological measures, measurement scales, **questionnaires**, interviews, observations and documentary sources. The chapter will not discuss the ways in which any information collected through measurement could be analysed, as this is fully considered in Chapter 9.

Physiological and psychological measures

Both physiological and psychological measures are important to health and social care practice. Both types of measures are used on a day-to-day basis to record patient and client information. Many of these measures provide valuable information for the health and social care team, and, as valid and reliable measuring tools, they are often used by researchers .There are a variety of measuring instruments available to the researcher, including electronic tools. The range of valid and reliable physiological measures available is too vast to list. Examples include: the electronic Dinamap that records blood pressure; measurements of nerve impulses; digital and tympanic thermometers that record temperature; Clinitests that indicate urine composition; and biochemical tests that measure blood composition.

Many of these measures have been employed in the collection of research information and have been the subject of research that has considered the reliability of temperature recording tools. For example, Farnell, Maxwell, Tan, Rhodes and Philips (2005) assessed the accuracy and reliability of two non-invasive methods of temperature measurement in an intensive care environment. One hundred and sixty temperature sets from 25 adults were recorded using chemical (Tempa Dot™) and tympanic thermometers (Genius™ First Temp M3000A) and compared against the gold standard pulmonary artery catheter. The findings suggested the chemical thermometer was more accurate and reliable when compared with the tympanic thermometer. However, compared with the pulmonary artery catheter both methods gave erroneous recordings.

There are many psychological measures available to the researcher. For example, the State Trait Anxiety Inventory measures anxiety that increases as a result of threat (state anxiety), and anxiety that is an inherent part of the person's personality (trait anxiety). The measure offers a useful way of recording anxiety level which has been used by many researchers. Ng, Sham, Tang and Fung (2004) used the inventory to record maternal anxiety levels related to the Severe Acute Respiratory Syndrome (SARS) epidemic in Hong Kong. This study involved 980 pregnant women, with the results suggesting the SARS epidemic had brought drastic changes to the lives of people in Hong Kong.

The researcher needs to select the most appropriate physiological and psychological instruments to use in the research, which should be both valid and reliable measures. In preparation for data collection, the functioning and availability of equipment will need to be considered. Training in data collection methods, including use of equipment, must be complete before data collection can commence.

Measurement scales

Polit and Beck (2006) suggest a scale is a device which allows the assignment of numerical scores to a continuum measuring attributes, such as the scale that measures weight, the scale that measures shoe size or the scale that records height. Many scales are used generally in society. Within health and social care, scales are used to measure specific phenomena, and are important to daily practice. Such scales may, for example, measure pain response, nutritional status, risk of pressure sore development, and client satisfaction.

There are many valid and reliable scales available for use in health and social care research (Oppenheim, 1992; Bowling, 2002), many of which are used in practice. Oppenheim (1992) suggests the researcher may be able to select existing scales that would achieve the desired research outcome, provided copyright is sought. This overcomes validity and reliability issues that can arise when designing a new measuring scale, which would need to be tried and tested before use.

Scales may be the sole data collection instrument used by the researcher, or may be one of many data collection tools employed. Scales may also be included within the design of questionnaires (see later). Within this chapter the rating scale, **Likert scale** and Visual Analogue Scale, **repertory grid** and **vignettes** are considered.

Rating scales are used to attribute a numerical score to an assessment or judgement (Oppenheim, 1992). The respondent is asked a question and then is guided to select from a series of numbered statements the one that reflects their assessment or judgement. The rating scale can be used to rate client satisfaction with the quality of care received. The client may be asked, for example, to assess the quality of information giving, and grade the information given in relation to a scale of 0–5, with 0 being unsatisfactory and 5 being completely satisfactory.

The scale may be used for example, in gathering information from elderly residents about their care environment, as in Figure 8.1.

Burns and Grove (2005) suggest rating scales can be easy to generate, and offer a useful form of measurement provided the end statements are not so extreme as to affect their selection.

		Rating
Please rate from 1(low) – 10 (high), the following statements in relation to your care.		
1	Quietness during the day	( )
2	Quietness during the night	( )
3	Choice of food	( )
4	Heating	( )
5	Bathroom facilities	( )
6	Attitude of staff	( )
7	Provision of social facilities	( )
8	Cleanliness of the residence	( )
9	Comfort of the bed	( )

Figure 8.1 *Example of a Rating Scale*

The scales are, however, crude measures, and the information generated in this way is limited. In the example above, the attitude of staff may be rated in relation to one poor experience or one very positive experience; in other words, the client's response can be swayed by one event, rather than reflecting a general impression.

The Likert scale is a commonly used scale. Named after psychologist Rensis Likert, it is used to obtain attitude or opinion to ten or more statements. The scale is a more refined tool that forces the respondent to give opinion on a series of statements, indicating whether they: strongly disagree, disagree, are neutral or unsure, agree, strongly agree. Usually the scale includes five values, to which numerical scores can be ascribed. More commonly, a high score (5) is achieved by agreement with a positively worded statement and disagreement with a negative statement (Polit and Beck 2006). Figure 8.2 gives an example of this.

In Figure 8.2, the response to statement one receives a score of 5, as the respondent strongly agrees with a positive statement. If

	Strongly agree	Agree	Neutral	Disagree	Strongly disagree	Score
1 Children behaving badly benefit from individual attention	✓					5
2 Children behaving badly do not benefit from individual attention	✓					1

Figure 8.2   *An example of a Likert scale used to measure attitude to discipline in children*

the respondent had strongly disagreed with the positive statement, a score of 1 would be allocated. The response to statement two receives a score of 1, as the respondent has strongly agreed to a negative statement. To strongly disagree to this statement would achieve a score of 5.

The scale should be composed of equal numbers of negative and positive statements. If the scale included only positive statements, it would be easy for the respondent to select only positive responses, agreeing with all the statements without thought. There is the potential for respondents to continually choose neutral responses and thus give no impression of attitude or opinion. Respondents might also give the response that meets current 'no smacking' thinking.

Other methods of assessing attitudes include repertory grids and vignettes. The repertory grid is a technique used by the researcher to elicit an individual's constructs (perceptions) concerning specific issues through deep exploration of the individual's perceptions, expressed in their own words. Further explanations of the technique can be seen in Bowling (2002).

Vignettes are short descriptions of a topic of interest, event, situation, scenario or case history, which are presented to respondents with a series of structured questions. Vignettes are most commonly written descriptions, though can be video tapes, that are used to gain information about the respondent's perceptions, opinions or knowledge about a situation (Polit

Figure 8.3   *Visual Analogue Scale*

and Beck, 2006; Bowling 2002). Spalding (2004) used a vignette portraying a patient awaiting a hip replacement to encourage health care professionals to reflect on their practice and implement changes. The research outcomes suggested that the use of the vignette had supported multi-professional reflections.

The Visual Analogue Scale is a vertical or horizontal line, showing a scale measuring 0–100 mm, with each millimetre representing a numerical score (Polit and Beck 2006). The end points of the scale symbolise extreme values, with the line denoting all values between. The measurement of pain experience can be achieved using a scale with end points representing unbearable pain and no pain, with all other pain experiences being found along the scale. When using the scale, the patient marks along the line the point which they feel represents their current pain response (see Figure 8.3).

In constructing the scale, the values used to identify the end points need consideration, as they need to reflect extremes. There may also be potential difficulties in obtaining a true response. In the example above, patients may be reluctant to admit to having unbearable pain. Panditi and Silverman (2003) used a Visual Analogue Scale to explore perceptions of exercise induced asthma amongst children and their parents. The scale was constructed with the ends marked as 'very bad' and 'no problem at all', noting the two extremes.

In selecting measurement scales the researcher will need to know which scales are available and feel confident that the scales used will be sensitive enough to obtain the responses required. In addition, the researcher will need to know that the scales are valid and reliable measures.

Questionnaires

The questionnaire is the most frequently used data collection instrument. It is composed of a series of written questions which usually require written responses. The questionnaire can be used to collect information that is amenable to statistical analysis, and it can therefore be used to collect data in quantitative studies.

The questionnaire offers the researcher flexibility in its delivery as it can be administered by hand to individuals, to groups of people, or can be posted or emailed to reach a large number of people across a wide geographical area. It is often, therefore, the data collection instrument chosen for use in surveys. In addition, the questionnaire can be completed anonymously, which can be of value in research studies where honest opinion is sought, or in situations of unequal researcher and respondent status. For example, questionnaires can be useful in collecting information from service users as part of auditing the quality of care being delivered by a particular service or professional. The questionnaire proved valuable in overcoming difficulties when dental patients formed a dentist's research sample (White, Slabber and Schreuder, 2001), and in collecting sensitive information about sexual risk behaviours of heterosexual black African American women living with HIV disease (Whyte and Dawson, 2001).

Whilst reviewing the literature, the researcher may identify a questionnaire that would be an appropriate tool for use in the research study. With the original author's consent, it would be possible to use the same or slightly modified instrument and thus save valuable time in questionnaire generation.

The construction of a new questionnaire requires skill and can be time consuming. The questionnaire must include questions that will elicit responses needed to address the research question. This process involves using skill and knowledge in questionnaire design. In addition, the researcher must establish the validity and reliability of the instrument, using the instrument to collect data, perhaps as part of a pilot study (see Chapter 3).

When formulating a questionnaire, the researcher makes decisions about its structure and layout. The main types of question included are open or closed. Open questions require a response of one or more words or sentences. For example, the question, 'In your own words, describe what social care is', would probably be answered in a few sentences. Closed questions are structured to offer the respondent a choice of answers. The scales discussed earlier might be used within this structure. An example of a closed question is seen in Figure 8.4

Please tick the appropriate response:

1   Sex

	Male	( )01
	Female	( )02

2   Length of experience in professional role

	1–3 years	( )01
	4–6 years	( )02
	7–10 years	( )03
	11–15 years	( )04
	16–20 years	( )05
	20+ years	( )06

Figure 8.4   *An example of closed questions with coded responses*

Questions should not be leading, such as, 'You don't support this new idea do you?', nor should they be value laden or ask more than one question at a time. One example of this is the commonly used question, 'Do you want a cup of tea and do you want a biscuit?', which is in fact asking two questions at once. The organisation of questions is also important. Asking sensitive questions at the beginning of the questionnaire can adversely affect response rates. It is usual to establish personal details, and ask general questions first, before moving on to more specific and directed questions. The researcher will also need to allow sufficient space to enable the respondent to give full answers.

Instructions for completion of the questionnaire need to be clear, particularly as the researcher is often not available to clarify any queries. The researcher should include a covering letter of introduction, in which response deadlines may be set and incentives may be offered. It is not uncommon for researchers to offer material reward to those completing a questionnaire.

As part of questionnaire construction the researcher must consider data analysis. Closed questions might be coded, as shown in Figure 8.4. In question 1, the codes 01 and 02 relate to the sex of the respondents. These codes would be used to prepare the data for analysis. Analysis of open questions would be concerned with identifying specific content, and thus forms part of **content analysis,** which is discussed as part of data analysis in Chapter 9.

The potential benefits of using a questionnaire to collect research data relate to the effective use of researcher time, reduced costs, access to a world wide sample, access to a large sample at one time, **anonymity,** and reduced researcher bias. The potential drawbacks can include difficulties in questionnaire construction and exclusion of certain sample groups, such as children and those with language or learning difficulties. There is the potential to alienate certain groups from the research if a barrier such as availability of questionnaires in different languages is not considered. Furthermore, the researcher may receive unexpected responses but is unable to pursue these further as the individual respondents are not identified.

The expected respondent may not complete the questionnaire, and additional disadvantages might include unsatisfactory completion, rendering the questionnaire useless and spoilt. Response rates can be poor, with mailed questionnaires often achieving a 25–30% response (Burns and Grove, 1999). If a response of less than 50% is achieved, the representativeness of the sample can be called into question (Burns and Grove,1999). Booth, Booth and Falzon (2003) used a postal questionnaire to sample social care practitioners, including social workers and occupational therapists. The questionnaires asked about their attitudes to evidence-based practice, access to information and their training requirements. The overall response rate was 27%, which was disappointingly low and called into question the representativeness of the sample.

When response appears low, it is accepted that researchers will follow up the sample with reminders, either by post or email. Response to postal questionnaires is also aided by providing stamped and addressed reply envelopes, as well as including reply dates as part of an introductory letter, as mentioned earlier. If administered by hand, the researcher might collect the questionnaires or organise a collection point, which will aid response.

Interviews

Interviews are the second most frequently used data collection technique, which involves the collection of information by verbal communication. Interviews can be conducted on an individual basis either face-to-face or over the telephone, or within a group setting. The interview can be used in qualitative research, to collect in-depth information from which theory can be generated. An interview may also form part of a quantitative design, when a structured interview schedule is used.

The interview schedule is constructed using many of the principles of questionnaire design (see earlier) and includes a list of questions to be posed. The researcher works systematically through the schedule, recording responses. This format can be used in a face-to-face interview or in a telephone interview. Jegermalm (2004) used telephone interviews to collect data from informal carers in a Swedish county. The results showed that few carers received any support that directly related to their role. Structuring the interview facilitated consistency in data collection.

Face-to-face interviews can be less structured, with the researcher identifying one or more key questions that can give some organisation to the interview. The researcher, ultimately allowing the respondent to give direction to the interview, can explore individual responses to the questions. This open design can yield in-depth information about people's opinions, attitudes and feelings, and can be used in individual or group interviews.

The focus group is composed of 6 to 12 members of differing opinion, who meet to discuss research issues (Bowling, 2002). The group discussion can last from one to three hours and is based on outline questions generated through literature review. The facilitator poses the questions or statements and records the group discussion. The focus group can provide a useful forum for discussing a range of topics, offering the researcher rich data from which further research questions can be generated.

The researcher must decide which interview design will enable the collection of data needed to address the research question. Questions used in an interview must be constructed following the principles of question formation (see Questionnaires earlier in this Chapter). In particular the content of questions and the organisation of questions need consideration.

As interviews necessitate verbal interaction, the researcher needs to consider how to gain access to the sample, making arrangements to conduct interviews at a time convenient to the respondent. The researcher must also consider the duration of the interview, with 45 minutes being a realistic maximum participation time. These points would apply if the interview were conducted over the telephone or face-to-face. The researcher needs a suitable environment for the interview, with privacy and quietness being important considerations.

The recording of an interview may or may not involve the use of technology. Long hand written recording of interviewee responses is often used and can be preferred by respondents who may object to being electronically recorded. However, the researcher might find it useful to record an interview on cassette, disc or videotape. This facilitates analysis of content as the researcher can listen to the interview several times and, if videoed, may be able to identify non-verbal communication more easily. Audio recordings can be transcribed more readily, which will also aid analysis. The researcher may ask a second person to view or listen to recordings, to help with the analysis process. In obtaining a second viewpoint, the researcher may be alerted to new information that had been overlooked, may be forced to re-examine their perceptions of the interview, and help validate the findings, thus improving analysis.

Interviewing is a skill that is often presumed to be innate. It is, however, a skill that needs developing, as is depicted by many experienced television interviewers. The researcher is therefore likely to use the pilot study to test the interview schedule or questions, as well as to develop interviewing skills. The interviewer must consider habits, such as nodding or smiling, used in asking questions as the interviewee might identify these as cues to the sort of response that is wanted. The interviewer has the potential to bias the results in many ways, such as through non-verbal and verbal cues, and by the nature of the relationship with the respondent. A researcher in a perceived position of power may not receive true responses, and a researcher seen to be of lower status than the respondent may be dealt with in a dismissive way by the interviewee.

Guaranteeing anonymity might overcome some of the difficulties encountered when trying to gain truthful information from respondents. There are special considerations when using vulnerable groups, such as those with mental health problems as the research sample. The researcher will need to be confident that the respondents are enabled to divulge their true feelings and opinions, and acknowledge that the results may be affected by the person's dependency or vulnerability.

Interviews provide a flexible data collection tool, which can allow the researcher to explore pertinent issues raised during the course of the interview. The interview can provide detailed information, and may also be useful in collecting data from groups unable to respond to a questionnaire, such as children. The organisation of interviews requires thought and organisation. Interviews are also more time consuming, with each interview possibly taking about 45 minutes, 30 minutes of which is spent collecting data. Interviewer bias and the researcher–respondent relationship may affect the quality of the information collected.

Observations

Observational studies collect information from observing behaviours or events. Information collected in this way is not often numerical, but is a written record of the researcher's interpretation of events, and is therefore a method that is employed mostly in qualitative research. Observational studies can record the complexity of health and social care, which may not easily be measured using any self-reporting methods, such as interviews and questionnaires. However, there are a number of ethical issues associated with this research method, requiring the researcher to operate in an open way adopting an 'overt role' as either participant or **non-participant observer.**

The participant observer is part of the situation under observation and needs to maintain a clinical role whilst recording data, which may prove problematic. The non-participant observer would be identified as a researcher, perhaps sitting in a sports centre observing the use of the swimming facilities. The researcher would need some insight and knowledge of the events observed to interpret observations made. The researcher assuming a non-participant role may use more structured data collection tools, such as an observation schedule. The schedule would be predetermined, allowing recording of events under observation in a structured way. For example, the schedule might record verbal interactions with a group of patients on the ward. This would necessitate the recording with whom the

Time/Patient	Alan	Perry	Miles	Tony	Ken
0900 hours	A,D	N	C	/	L
0905	/	N	M	I	L
0910	/	N	M	/	L
0915	G,E,F,D	N	B,C	/	L
0920	E,D	G,E, F,D	/	/	L
0925	E,D	/	G,E, F,D	O	N

Key	
A = health care assistant	I = ward clerk
B = student nurse	J = relatives
C = staff nurse	K = other patients
D = sister/charge nurse	L = dietician
E = house officer	M = physiotherapist
F = registrar	N = occupational therapist
G = consultant	O = social worker
H = domestic	P = other

Figure 8.5   *An example of an observation schedule used to record verbal interaction with patients*

interactions are made, and the time taken to complete conversation. The researcher would use codes to identify all possible personnel involved to facilitate easy recording. The end result might appear as in Figure 8.5.

To achieve consistency in measurement, there needs to be parity in the recording and interpretation of information. This can be achieved using recording techniques and through training the observer. In some instances it may be useful to have more than one observer to overcome difficulties with observer reliability and bias. For example, Odd, Page, Battin and Harding (2004) used two observers to independently review radiographs taken to identify the positioning of percutaneous central venous lines placed in neonates. The observers' interpretations of the films were tested and found to be reliable.

Recording information gained through observation can pose difficulty for the researcher. A non-participant observer might use an observation schedule, as discussed earlier, or a one-way mirror, or may even record events on video for later analysis. The participant observer needs to either memorise events or find some way of recording field notes.

Access to the sample can also be more problematic. The researcher must organise access to the environment and needs to consider time-management, as it is possible that observations may take from days to weeks or months. There are many issues surrounding the potential effects observational studies may have on the sample, as such studies can be more invasive and obtrusive.

Observations can be problematic to the participants, requiring changes to accommodate either researcher or data collection instruments. The constant presence of researchers or data collection instruments may also affect the quality of observation. The 'Hawthorne' effect is a well-documented account of the effect of researcher presence on the research outcomes. In the study, researchers, considering how to increase productivity at an electrical plant, made recommendations based on the increase in productivity seen during their research, which changed heating, light and rest time. These recommendations were adopted by the managers who then saw production fall. Researcher presence had therefore led to a temporary increase in production. The researcher can, therefore, introduce bias to the observations, by affecting the events observed.

Recording the data relates to the observer role adopted. The non-participant observer may use an observation schedule and find concentration on events easier than the participant observer. There may, however, be ethical dilemmas for the researcher to cope with. For example, if a nurse researcher is recording events in a ward area when a cardiac arrest occurs, there may be personal dilemma between continuing the observer role and the need to react as a nurse to the situation. This is sometimes called the 'dual role' of researcher/practitioner.

The participant observer may have difficulties recording information, though the information gained may be more insightful. Additional problems may arise if the researcher becomes subsumed into the culture, which might affect their objective interpretation of the situation.

Observational studies can provide an in-depth understanding of events, particularly if the researcher has experienced the subject of the research. Often observation may be the only technique available to collect the information needed. However, observational methods rely on the researcher's perceptions and interpretations of events, and are therefore open to individual bias. There are also ethical and organisational issues to consider, including access, recording data, role adoption and management of time. Observations can offer the researcher information, which might not be obtained using self-reporting techniques, and this is particularly evident when considering behaviour and events.

Documentary evidence

Existing documents are a rich source of research information that form part of **secondary data** collection techniques. Researchers may be able to access and interpret many health and social care documents, such as case notes, census data, care pathways, minutes of committee meetings, policy papers and letters. This facilitates analysis of existing material that has been collected for a purpose other than research, which is identified as secondary data.

Other types of documentary evidence have been used in many research studies. Moule (2005) describes the use of diaries as one of three data collection methods in research that explored whether health care students working online as part of an interprofessional module could develop a community of learners. The diaries provided a useful individual record of student experience throughout the module.

The increased recording of documentary information in health care is likely to provide greater impetus for its use in research. Secondary data sources are likely to gain popularity in the research field as data recording improves, and the reduced costs and time involved in using existing documentary sources will also be factors affecting their future use (Bowling, 2002).

Other considerations in using documentary evidence relate to researcher bias, which may be reduced if someone else has completed the initial recording of information. However, relying on data collected by others can bring its own problems, as when, for instance, records are rendered useless because of initial recording problems. Records may be incomplete, inaccurate, or lacking in data needed for research analysis. When analysing secondary data, prior to undertaking the study, the researcher must establish the existence and authenticity of records relevant to the research. Access to relevant records must be negotiated, and sampling issues considered to overcome sampling bias (see Chapter 7).

Consideration must also be given to the analysis of information that was collected within one context that is to be used by the researcher in another context to address a research question. It is possible that analysis by the researcher will ignore the context in which the data were originally collected and inappropriate judgements may be made. Jacobson, Hamilton and Galloway (1993) suggest that the secondary analyst can misinterpret findings and draw invalid conclusions.

The increased need to record information in health care offers the researcher a wealth of information for consideration. The potential gains from such analysis have been recognised by many researchers and are likely to be considered by many more in the future, despite the potential difficulties which arise from using and analysing secondary data.

Triangulation of data collection

Researchers often employ more than one methodological approach, using multiple methods to collect data. The term 'triangulation of methods' is used to imply that three or more research methods have been used in one study, often involving both **quantitative** and **qualitative data collection** methods (Gilbert, 2001). For example, data collection might include using a questionnaire with closed and open questions to ascertain client use of a new service, followed by focus group interviews and analysis of individual diaries. Moule (2005) discussed above, employed individual interviews, online diary collection and the analysis of data collected from online discussion board data within one study. The use of multiple methods of data collection is more commonly seen in health and social care research, allowing researchers to access a range of data to address research questions set.

Key Points

- Research information can be collected in many ways.
- The research approach taken will influence the choice of data collection instruments.
- Reliability and validity are important qualities of any data collection instrument.
- Establishing trustworthiness should be considered in qualitative research.
- Methods of analysis will need consideration prior to data collection.

Further Reading

Bell, J. (2005). *Doing your research project: a guide for first-time researchers in education, health and social science* (4th ed.). Buckingham: Open University Press.

Bowling, A. (2002). *Research methods in health: investigating health and health services* (2nd ed.). Buckingham: Open University Press.

Burns, N. and Grove, S. (1999). *Understanding nursing research* (2nd ed.). Philadelphia: W. B. Saunders and Company. Chapter 9.

Burns, N. and Grove, S. (2005). *The practice of nursing research: conduct, critique and utilization* (5th ed.). St. Louis, MO: Elsevier Saunders.

McDowell, I. and Newell, L. (1987). *Measuring health: a guide to rating scales and questionnaires.* Oxford: Oxford University Press.

Nurse Researcher (1998). *Healthcare assessment tools,* 5 (3), Spring.

Oppenheim, A. (1992). *Questionnaire design, interviewing and attitude measurement* (2nd ed.). London: Pinter Publishers.

Parahoo, K. (2006). *Nursing research: principles, process and issues* (2nd ed.). Basingstoke: Palgrave.

Polit, D. and Beck, C. (2006). *The essentials of nursing research: methods, appraisal and utilization* (6th ed.). Philadelphia: Lippincott Williams and Wilkins.

9 Making Sense of Data Analysis

Learning Outcomes

On completion of this chapter the reader should be able to:

- understand the difference between descriptive and inferential statistics
- identify the significance of quantitative results
- appreciate the steps required to complete qualitative data analysis.

Key Terms

- standard deviation ▪ measures of central tendency ▪ levels of measurement ▪ constant comparison ▪ thematic analysis ▪ parametric ▪ non-parametric ▪ normal distribution ▪ grounded theory

Introduction

Many professionals and students in health and social care find the results and analysis section of a research article difficult to understand. This chapter is aimed at demystifying some of the terminology used in those sections and helping those who read and interpret the findings of published research.

The type of analysis the researcher can apply to the data varies according to the approach taken, and nature of data collected. **Quantitative data analysis** is discussed in the first part of the chapter and emphasis placed on the interpretation of results. In the discussion on **qualitative data analysis** the core methods used by researchers from the various qualitative approaches will be identified and examples from current health and social care research used to illustrate points made.

Data analysis used in quantitative research studies

Descriptive statistics

When a researcher plans their research design they must have some idea of the type of data analysis that will match their approach to the study and the data collecting methods employed. In the first part of the data analysis section of a research article, the researcher usually makes an attempt to describe their results and put them in the context of all the responses obtained.

When we are asked to describe the age of a group of people, one way we could do it is to give an 'average' age of the group. This is something we use in many contexts of our everyday life. Averages of different kinds are used in research articles to describe a set of responses. The type of average used depends on the type of data the researcher is working with.

Below are two questions from a questionnaire which asked students how they had travelled to university that morning, and also the distance they had travelled.

1 Please tick the box which identifies how you travelled to college this morning

Car	☐	Bus	☐	Motorcycle	☐
Train	☐	Bicycle	☐	Walk	☐
Other	☐				

2 Please identify to the nearest kilometre the distance you travelled to university this morning

These two questions will produce quite different types of data, and because of that will need different kinds of averages. In question one, the researcher will need to add up all the respondents who ticked each of the boxes and could end up with a list such as this:

Car	64	Bus	11	Motorcycle	5
Train	0	Bicycle	7	Walk	8
Other	0				

To tell us something about the way this group of students travelled to university the researcher will have to identify the means of transport used by most students. In this case that will be car, with 64 – the most common by a long way. In statistical terms this type of data is called nominal as it is collected in named categories (for example, car, train), and the researcher counts the frequency found in each category. The category that occurs most frequently is called the **mode**. If two categories have the same frequency the data is called bi-modal, and with more than two categories the term multi-modal is used.

In question two, the respondents are asked to provide the distance they travelled to university. This is potentially an accurate measurement in which the scale used (kilometres) is recognised internationally. If one student travelled two kilometres it would be acknowledged that a student who travelled four kilometres had travelled twice as far. To tell us about the distances travelled to university by the students the researcher could calculate the average as we use it in our everyday lives; that is, add all the distances and divide that sum by the number of students. In statistical terms this type of data is called ratio, and the average referred to as the **mean**.

In between these two categories of data are two more. Ordinal data are measurements which can be put into a rank order but are not measured on an accurate scale. This means that the researcher could put the data in order from lowest to highest or smallest to largest but that is all. A good example of this type of data is the scale used in the assessment of patient's pain. The score on a Visual Analogue Scale (see Chapter 8) used to measure a patient's pain is an example of ordinal data. If one patient marked six on such a scale it cannot be said that they have exactly twice the pain of a patient who marked three. However, it might be gauged that they were in more pain at the time.

Due to the inaccuracy of the measurement, a mean should not be used as an average in this type of measurement. Instead, to obtain a way of describing ordinal data, all the measurements are

Table 9.1   *Summary of levels of measurement and measures of central tendency (MCT)*

Date	Characteristics	MCT
Nominal	frequency of categories	mode
Ordinal	no scale but can be ranked	median
Interval	measured on a scale but no zero	mean
Ratio	most accurate, measured on scale with absolute zero	mean

put into a rank order, from lowest to highest or smallest to largest, and the middle measurement of the rank is identified as the **median**. So, for example, to describe the risk of re-offending of a group of young offenders the researcher would put the risk assessment scores of each young offender in a rank order, from lowest to highest, and find the score exactly in the centre. This would give some indication of the risk of re-offending held by a group of young offenders.

The final category of data that may be used is interval data. This is similar to ratio data but a scale is used in which there is no absolute zero and therefore no fixed point. The example usually given in statistical texts is that of the Fahrenheit scale for measuring temperature. However, as this data is measured on a recognised scale the mean is the average used. Usually in health and social care research interval and ratio data are treated together.

These different types of data are called levels of measurement and are regarded as a hierarchy. Statisticians refer to the averages which have been described as measures of central tendency. A summary of the levels of measurement and measures of central tendency are seen in Table 9.1.

When using interval or ratio data, researchers can go further in their ability to describe the data recorded from their sample. They can show if their sample had very similar scores, or if their scores covered a wide range. To do this the data must be put in a format where not only is the mean identified, but also the number of respondents who achieved each score is also identified. Statisticians have found that if they take any measurement from a random sample of subjects there will always be a few at the extremes of a measurement scale but most will be clustered around the mean. This is easiest shown in a diagram. Figure 9.1 shows a normal distribution curve; that is, a pattern

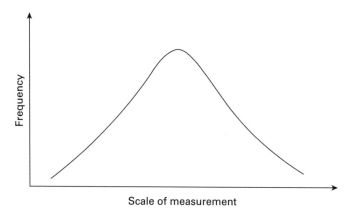

Figure 9.1   *Normal distribution curve*

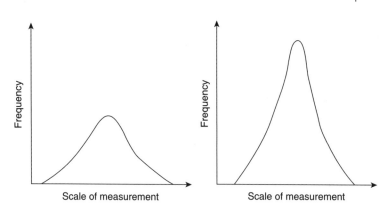

Figure 9.2   *Different distribution curves*

of measurements, shaped like a bell, in which the horizontal axis is the scale of measurements and the vertical axis is the frequency of each of the measurements.

This bell shape can vary between being short and fat and tall and thin (see Figure 9.2).

The shape of the bell can tell us quite a lot about a set of results and therefore about a sample. To illustrate this look at Figure 9.3.

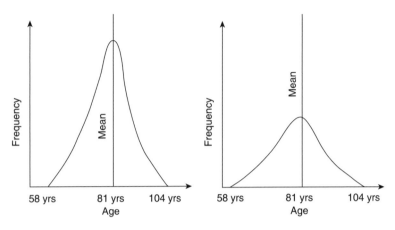

Figure 9.3   *Bell-shaped curve – patient/age distribution on elderly care ward*

The bell on the left shows the range of ages of patients admitted to a stroke rehabilitation unit the first year after it had opened. It can be seen that ages range from 58 years (the youngest) to 104 years (the oldest) and that the mean age was 81 years.

The bell on the right shows the range of ages of patients admitted to the same unit five years later. The range of ages remains much the same and so does the mean and yet the shape of the bell is very different. The tall thin bell on the left shows that the ages of a majority of patients were very close to the mean, with very few at the extremes of the age span. However, the bell on the right, shows that there were many more patients at the extremes, with far fewer patients clustered around the mean age of 81 years. When comparing these two distribution curves the researcher might begin to think of reasons why these results have been gained and the effect of these changes on the workload of the staff. Reasons for the change might include, for example, different admissions policy or other faculties in the community. The effect on the staff might include the need for a flexible approach to the use of a multi-disciplinary team.

When reading research articles the mean of a set of results might be given along with another figure called the **standard deviation** (sd). The standard deviation refers to the spread of

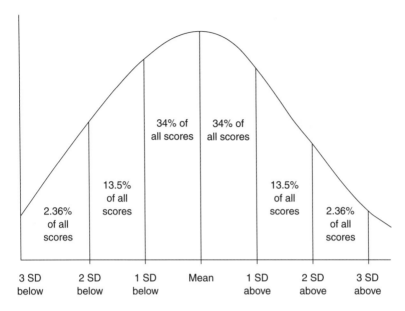

Figure 9.4   *Bell-shaped curve and standard deviation*

the results away from the mean. In other words, it is a numerical value given to the shape of the bell curve referred to above.
The value of the standard deviation is determined by calculating
the difference between each of the scores, and the mean and
then finding an average difference.

As standard deviation is calculated on the more rigorous
measurements of interval and ratio data, various assumptions
can be made from the use of a standard deviation and the bell
shaped curve. Figure 9.4 shows a normal distribution curve
with the standard deviation marked in. On each side of the
mean there is one standard deviation marked: on the left it is
minus one standard deviation and on the right, plus one standard deviation. This allows the researcher to predict, from the
sample, the number of the population who will 'fall between'
−1 and +1 and −2 and +2 standard deviation.

Sometimes the standard deviation is used to see if two groups
are comparable and can be used in further statistical testing. It
must be remembered that the standard deviations always read
in conjunction with the mean.

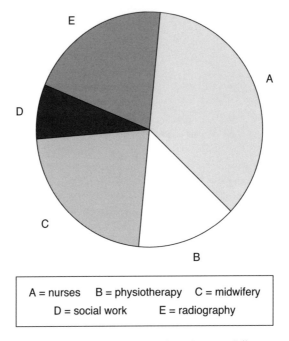

A = nurses   B = physiotherapy   C = midwifery
D = social work   E = radiography

Figure 9.5   *Pie chart showing groups of students as follows:*

It can be seen from Figure 9.4 that 68% of all cases will fall between −1 and +1 and 95% of the population between −2 and +2 standard deviation.

Another way researchers describe their results is with the aid of pictorial representation. Pie charts such as Figure 9.5 are used in nominal data to show the proportion of each category to the whole set of results.

Each slice of the pie represents one category. Sometimes the sections are simply drawn, but other times researchers will actually pull a slice of the pie out to make a particular point. A pie chart is an effective yet simple pictorial representation of a set of results which demonstrates how each segment is a proportion of a whole.

Another common representation used to describe a set of results is a bar chart. Bar charts are often used to compare differences between groups or changes in groups.

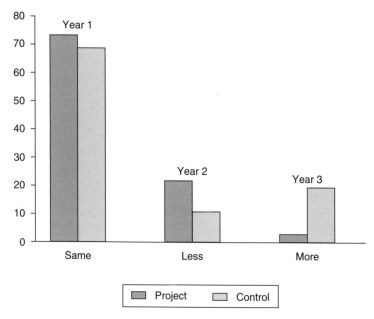

Figure 9.6   *Bar Chart comparison of teachers' stress (%) in a 'control' school and a project school over three years.*

When looking at both pie and bar charts, extremes of measurement should be noted, and the questioning process of why these results have occurred should be starting.

Figure 9.6 shows a bar chart used to describe the results of a study by Pritchard and Williams (2001) comparing the stress felt by teachers in a 'project' school looking at reducing their stress, and those in a 'control' school.

Having described a set of results many researchers attempt to put some meaning into them. When reading a research article, this part of the data analysis usually follows the **descriptive statistics** and uses **inferential statistics,** or statistics which infer some meaning.

Inferential statistics

In quantitative studies the researcher frequently looks for a relationship between two or more variables, or a difference between two or more groups. The statistical tests which are used reflect this.

Tests of a relationship (in statistical terms referred to as a correlation) are chosen according to the level of measurement of the data. The two most common correlation tests are Spearman's Rank Correlation used for ordinal data and Pearson Product Moment used on interval or ratio data. The symbols used to denote these two tests are R_s for Spearman's and r for Pearson. Regardless of the actual test used, a coefficient or figure will be calculated which shows if there is a relationship between the variables, and, if so, how strong that relationship is. A positive correlation indicates that as the measurement of one variable has increased, so has the measurement on the other variable. A correlation coefficient between +0.6 and +0.9 shows a strong positive relationship. The closer the figure is to +1 the stronger the relationship. Similarly a **correlation coefficient** between –0.6 and –0.9 shows a strongly negative relationship. This indicates that as one measurement has increased the other has decreased. A correlation coefficient either side of 0 suggests that there is either a very loose relationship or no relationship between the variables. In their study investigating the experience of verbal abuse of nurses in a large hospital, Sofield and Salmond (2003) found a positive correlation between the amount of abuse received and intent to leave nursing practice (r = 0.24), though not a strongly positive one.

Sometimes a correlation coefficient is obtained to demonstrate reliability between two researchers who are working together. Tests of inter-rater reliability are one way in which a researcher can demonstrate the robust nature of the measurements in a quantitative study. Two researchers will independently take measurements of the same variable and compare their results. It is expected that the correlation will be over r = 0.80.

There are many different statistical tests of difference used by researchers in their attempt to demonstrate significant findings in their results. As in the measurement of central tendency and the correlation tests, the choice of tests that can be used depends on the level of measurement of the data. Tests which can be used on nominal and ordinal data are referred to as non-parametric, and are less powerful than those used on interval and ratio data which are called **parametric tests**. To be used, parametric tests usually need data which have a normal distribution, with samples having similarly shaped bell curves.

The most common statistical test used on nominal data is chi squared (χ^2). **Non-parametric tests** which can be used on ordinal data, and look at the difference in the ranking of a data set, include the Mann Whitney U test and the Wilcoxon test. Parametric tests which are frequently seen in research literature include the t-test and ANOVA (Analysis of Variance). A further consideration the researcher has when deciding which test to use lies in the number of groups included in the study.

To be able to interpret quantitative research data it is not necessary to have an in-depth knowledge of these tests although it is necessary to understand why the tests are performed, and how the results can be interpreted. All the tests (both parametric and non-parametric) produce a number – an index, usually with an initial before it such as U or t. These initials simply identify the statistical test which was used. Most commonly the data are entered into a statistical computer package (often SPSS). The result produced by the computer looks as follows

$$p < 0.05, p < 0.01, p < 0.001$$

The p stands for probability and it gives the researcher an insight into how significant their results are, and what the probability is that the results occurred by chance. Users of research also need to know how powerful research results are; they are rarely interested in results which could have happened by chance, or were a 'one off'. The three probability values listed are sometimes referred to as critical values, as they are the levels of significance most frequently quoted in health and social care research:

- $p < 0.05$ – is the least powerful result usually accepted as significant in health and social care research. It means five times out of a hundred these results could have occurred by chance.
- $p < 0.01$ – is a more acceptable level and refers to a one in a hundred likelihood of the result occurring by chance.
- $p < 0.001$ – is a highly significant result and the odds of these results occurring by chance has dropped to one in a thousand.

When the result is followed by ns it means that the result is non-significant. The use of these results is illustrated in a study by Pritchard and Williams (2001) who completed a **longitudinal study** of a school-based social work family service to reduce truancy, delinquency and school exclusions. In a comparison of stress felt by teachers in a 'project' school compared to those in a control school the result was p<0.05 demonstrating that the teachers in the project school felt less stress than their counterparts. The data is nominal and the chi squared test was used to examine the difference in the two groups of teachers' stress scores. The computer generated the following significant result – $\chi^2 = 15.77$ p < 0.05. Thus the null hypothesis that there would be no difference in the stress levels of the two groups of teachers could be rejected. The researchers could conclude that the teachers in the 'project' school felt less stress than their counterparts in the control school.

Similarly, in a study by Giles and Moule (2004) nurses' attitudes to, and experiences of, do not attempt resuscitation (DNAR) policy, were compared with five variables (age, grade, years of nursing, area and length of experience on current ward). Although the comparison between the variables and nurses' attitudes to DNAR decision-making was non-significant (ns), when the researchers compared the nurses' experiences of DNAR decision-making there was a significant difference found when compared to area of practice (p < 0.01). Nurses working in acute and general medical wards had better experiences of DNAR decision-making than colleagues did in general surgical, neurosurgical and orthopaedics/trauma.

The more research is read, including these statistical results, the more familiar the terminology will become. This part of the chapter has attempted to introduce some of the issues in quantitative data analysis in a way to help health and social care workers of all levels begin to feel more confident in reading statistical results. For a useful text on statistics see Scott and Mazhindu (2005).

Data analysis used in qualitative research studies

In Chapter 5 it was identified that there are several qualitative approaches to research including phenomenology, ethnography and grounded theory. In Chapter 8 the various research data collecting methods used in these types of research were discussed. However the data were collected, or whatever the exact approach used, eventually the researcher will work on the written word. Following data collection, the researcher will need to transcribe taped interview recordings, and complete observation field notes. The data from open questions on a questionnaire will be ready to work on.

The first task of the researcher is to try to put the data into some order. This is usually done by reading and re-reading the data, and identifying some preliminary categories which emerge. While selecting these categories there is a sense that the researcher needs to both tell a story, and paint a full picture of the topic under investigation. To do that the researcher must be careful in their choice of categories. Fielding (2001a) cites Silvey (1975) when she identifies that all research is about making comparisons of some sort. In order to make those comparisons the data must be organised into some form that allows comparisons to be made. At the preliminary stages of qualitative data analysis, a colleague may be asked to read a sample of the data and identify categories. There will then be some comparison of themes and an agreement sought.

Once the categories have been identified the data are scrutinised, and a coding scheme devised which incorporates all the categories found in the data. Robinson, Clare and Evans (2005) undertook an investigation into couples' psychological reactions to a diagnosis of dementia of one partner. From the analysis of the data the following themes arose: a) making sense and adjusting to loss, b) everything's changed, we have to go from there, c) not quite the same person. The actual coding might be completed in various ways. Some researchers mark the transcribed data with the code, while others cut up the pages of transcribed data and put the pieces of data for each code in a separate pile. Agar (1986, cited by Fielding, 1993) originated the analytical method of cutting up the data into strips, and literally pasting similarly coded strips onto pieces of card. The use of computer packages for qualitative analysis has eased the situation, although all the data have to first be fed into the computer using a word processor. The computer can then perform basic searches for the coded categories and allows retrieval of the coded segments. Three of the more common computer packages are ETHNOGRAPH, NUD*IST, ATLAS Ti and NVivo. An in-depth discussion of computer programmes for qualitative data analysis is found in Coffey, Holbrook and Atkinson (1996) and Gibbs (2002).

Once the data have been coded the next step is to look for common themes. These might be closely allied to the categories, or fall across the categories. Polit and Beck (2006) suggest that not only should themes be sought, but also patterns to the themes. Once these patterns have been identified the researcher might then be able to identify those themes that lie outside the patterns.

Sometimes the analysis may be completed using the constant comparative method. In this method, themes are identified early in the examination of the data, and then the rest of the data is scrutinised looking for the themes and constantly comparing the data with the themes. Further examples of constant comparison are found in the discussion of grounded theory (Glaser and Strauss, 1967; Strauss and Corbin, 1997).

In his discussion on the analysis of ethnographic data, Fielding (2001b) identifies that the researcher must be aware that not all data are equally important, and that some confidence must be shown over the selection of the data. Fielding continues to discuss the properties of 'good' qualitative analysis, in which there is a reflection of some truth about the phenomenon 'by reference to systematically gathered data' (Fielding, 2001b: 160). On the other hand, poor analysis that does not reflect the phenomenon is descriptive and lacking in any direction.

Unlike quantitative data analysis in which there is a need to generalise the results from a sample of the research population, qualitative data analysis does not demand **generalisability**. Rather, there is a quest to gain deeper understanding of the phenomenon under scrutiny.

Qualitative researchers attempt to increase the body of knowledge about certain phenomena. In some cases this involves examining data and identifying themes; however, other researchers plan to take their research further and actually develop theories from their data. Grounded theory, originated by Glaser and Strauss (1967), is frequently found in qualitative research. In these studies the constant comparison of themes begins soon after the first data are collected. Rather than collect the data in one stage, and then move on to the analysis as another stage, grounded theorists examine the early data straightaway, and then devise categories generated by the data to focus the rest of their data collection. As more data are collected, it is hoped they will reveal more about the categories, or cast doubt on the wisdom of their selection as categories. This part of the process is called theoretical sampling, and continues until the data fail to produce any new categories or information. To help validate the emerging theory, the categories may then be applied to a different, but similar setting, to see if it stands up to testing. This is referred to as comparative sampling, and allows the data to be utilised as a body of information constantly being updated and elaborated.

Content analysis

This system of analysis is almost like a bridge between qualitative and quantitative analysis, as there is some measurement involved. It is often used to analyse media coverage of a subject, although it can be used with any form of communication (for example, health promotion leaflets). When proceeding with this form of analysis, the researcher will first decide on the area of interest and then decide on the unit of analysis. This unit could be a word or centimetre of newsprint, or minutes of television coverage. It could be centimetres of newsprint devoted to headlines, compared to centimetres of newsprint devoted to the editorial. The other measurement employed might be the frequency with which a category appears within each unit of analysis. Some researchers will decide on a list of topics they want to examine, and simply sift through the data, making a note of whether or not the topic was included. Content analysis might be used to look at the information given to teenagers through the medium of 'teenage magazines'. The researcher would have first decided on a topic in which they were interested, for example, advice on contraception. A search of the available magazines would then be commenced, probably looking at a specific range of magazines over a specific length of time. Prior to searching the magazines the researcher would have decided on the themes they were looking for such as:

- the use of condoms
- clinics available for young people for advice
- need for safe sex and not just contraception;

or, the researcher might be interested in the mode in which any messages were conveyed, for example:

- whether the characters in the stories discuss sex or contraceptives
- whether there were editorials around the issue of contraception
- the context in which contraception was mentioned in the magazine.

Although not widely used as a means of analysis, content analysis is used in health education and promotion research, and offers a link between research and a means of communication. It is also used in forms of historical research, when the data are in the form of old documents including letters and reports.

Key Points

- Descriptive statistics describe results.
- Inferential statistics attempt to infer meaning from results.
- Different types of written questions produce different levels of measurement.
- The level of measurement of data dictates the measurement of central tendency and the statistical tests that can be used.
- Qualitative data analysis uses narrative to identify themes.
- In grounded theory the data collection and analysis are performed at the same time.

Further Reading

Bryan, A. and Cramer, D. (2005). *Quantitative data analysis with SPSS 12 and 13: a guide for social scientists.* London: Routledge.
Clegg, F. (1982). *Simple statistics.* Cambridge: Cambridge University Press.
Miles, M. and Huberman, M. (1994). *Qualitative data analysis: an expanded resource book* (2nd Ed.). Thousand Oaks: Sage.
Scott, I. and Mazhindu, D. (2005). *Statistics for healthcare professionals.* London: Sage.

10 Ethical Issues

Learning Outcomes

On completion of this chapter the reader should be able to:

- understand key ethical principles and rights related to research
- understand the nature of 'informed consent' for research participants
- discuss practitioners' responsibility to research participants
- identify the role of Research Ethics Committees
- understand the importance of Research Governance
- identify key issues when critically appraising the ethical aspects of research.

Key Terms

- ethical review
- confidentiality
- anonymity
- informed consent
- research governance
- code of conduct
- vulnerable participants
- ethical principles
- Research Ethics Committee

Introduction

More and more health and social care practitioners are becoming involved in practice-based research. Some are undertaking research projects as part of course work, and some health and social care practitioners work as research nurses, research physiotherapists, research fellows in social services, or as members of a multi-disciplinary research team. However, there are many more practitioners who are less directly involved in the whole process, perhaps through collecting data from patients and clients, such as administering client satisfaction questionnaires, collecting urine or blood samples, or collecting information for other research workers. Other people undertaking research could be social scientists, psychologists, health service researchers, and doctors. Whether a health and social care practitioner is the project leader, or a sole researcher, or collecting data for someone else, there are responsibilities with regard to the ethics and governance of research on humans. At all stages of the research process there are ethical implications, including the decision to undertake research or not, and the issue of undertaking poorly designed or executed research. Health and social care practitioners need to be aware of these issues in their own place of work.

Ethical principles

Ethical principles distinguish between socially acceptable behaviour from that which is considered socially unacceptable. There are a number of 'codes of conduct', or sets of principles and guidelines produced by professional and disciplinary bodies, such as the British Psychological Society, the British Sociological Association, the Royal College of Nursing, the General Medical Council. They all draw from the Declaration of Geneva, the Nuremberg Code and the Declaration of Helsinki: ethical guidelines produced as a result of human experimentation undertaken mainly during the Second World War. These build on basic human rights, now almost universally acknowledged.

The key ethical principles and basic human rights that should be followed throughout a research study in order to protect clients and patients are identified in Table 10.1

These principles and rights can be used as a framework to appraise research designs and methods and to examine the effects of research on the participants. It must be noted that some research designs will need to be considered in certain and more specific ways. For example, in some ethnographic studies, the participants may not know they are being observed and therefore have no choice about participating or not; in disseminating the research findings of action research, issues of **confidentiality** may be more difficult; in experimental research a random selection might result in a voluntary group who do not

Table 10.1   *Ethical principles and human rights in research*

The principle of veracity

- Telling the truth, being honest and being sincere.
- The right of participants to have full disclosure before participating in research.

The principle of justice

- Being fair to participants and not giving preference to some over others.
- Participants' needs must come before the objectives of the study.
- A duty to avoid discrimination, abuse or exploitation of the participants on the grounds of race, religion, sex, age, class or sexual orientation.

The principle of beneficence (or non-maleficence)

- The research should benefit both the individual participants, and society in general.
- A duty to do good and prevent harm (physical, psychological, social and economic).
- A duty of care to protect the weak and vulnerable.
- Defence of the weak, vulnerable or incompetent (advocacy role).

The principle of fidelity and respect

- The building of trust where the researcher is obliged to safeguard the welfare of participants.
- A duty to respect the rights, autonomy and dignity of participants.
- A duty to promote the well-being and autonomy of participants.
- The right to self-determination (the freedom to decide whether to participate or not, and to withdraw at any time).
- The right to privacy and respect.
- The right to anonymity and confidentiality.

represent the target population, being better educated, of a higher social class, more socially involved.

In addition to the methods and procedures used in research, the subject matter can also cause ethical concern, such as in the area of abuse or criminal activity, or with particularly vulnerable groups, such as the very old, or people with a severe learning disability or severe mental illness, or the dying. The challenge for readers of research, or those undertaking research in some way, is to maintain a balance between rigour and respect so that research evidence is produced ethically.

Informed consent

Informed consent is a concept familiar to many health and social care practitioners, particularly with reference to treatment and care. The principles of informed consent are also applied to patients and clients who are potential research participants and it is the fundamental ethical principle involved in research. There are a number of important considerations when research involves human volunteers, some of which have been discussed earlier: participants should know that they are taking part in research; they should give written informed consent to take part in the study; and they should be assured that they can withdraw at any time during the duration of the study. As part of providing information prior to participants giving consent, the researcher should also explain how and why participants were selected, and who is undertaking and financing the study. Written information might also include: an explanation of how long the study will take; whether there will be any discomfort; whether there are any conceivable risks or costs such as psychological or emotional distress resulting from self-disclosure; whether there may be any loss of privacy; and if there might be any loss of time or monetary costs associated with participating in the research. Likewise, participants should be informed of any potential benefits, such as material gains or comfort in being able to discuss their situation or escape from normal routine; knowledge that they may be helping others; and possibly enhanced self-esteem as a result of receiving special attention. Participants should also be given information about who to contact if they have any questions or complaints relating to the research. Written information should be given to the potential participants, and where possible they should be given time to consider whether they want to take part before seeking their written informed consent. Participants should have the power of free choice so that they are able to voluntarily consent or decline to participate in the research.

Vulnerable participants

Some people are considered to be vulnerable. They may be competent to give consent to participate, but may find it difficult to withhold consent if they are put under implicit or explicit pressure. People with learning disabilities, or who have a mental health problem, or are frail and elderly, or are living in an institution, may all be considered vulnerable, as may children and young people, and women who are pregnant because of hidden pressures or the risk of unintended side effects because of their particular circumstances. Including vulnerable people in research requires careful consideration as to exclude such groups from research may be a form of discrimination. Therefore, researchers need to justify why certain groups of people should be included in research, and consider not just the individual's ability to comprehend the information given, but as importantly the form and nature of the explanation given and the way that consent is obtained, particularly if participants are only intermittently competent to consent or have difficulty retaining information.

Some adults may not be competent to give consent. There must be clear justification for researchers including these groups of participants in research and it should never be undertaken if it could be equally undertaken with other adults. If a researcher wants to involve adults who are unable to give consent, it should be limited to the areas of research related to their incapacity. A researcher will also need to demonstrate that the research could be of direct benefit to, or improve knowledge of, their health or the health of people with the same state of health or same incapacity. The researcher must also establish that the individual has not expressed any objection either verbally or physically and that participation will not cause the participants emotional, physical or psychological harm.

Researchers may want to involve children and young people in research. However, as a potentially vulnerable group, they must not be exploited and may be unable to express their own needs, protect themselves from harm or make informed choices about being involved in research. If children and young people are not competent to independently give consent to participate in research, the consent of someone with parental responsibility must be obtained.

Health and social care practitioners must be fully aware of the issues surrounding informed consent. If a health and social care practitioner feels that a client or patient does not fully understand their role as a research participant, they have a responsibility to make this known to the researcher. Likewise, if the practitioner feels that a patient or client wishes to withdraw from a study, or that the research is having an adverse effect on the participants, they have a responsibility to make this known to an appropriate person in authority.

Confidentiality and anonymity

Participants in research have a right to expect that any information that they provide will be treated confidentially and that any disclosure of information about them will only be disclosed with their consent. There must be a clear understanding between the researcher and participant concerning the use to be made of the data provided, and how personal information will be stored.

Anonymity can be maintained by not using the names and addresses of participants, and assigning an identity number or code. The code to the names should be kept separately and securely so that the researcher cannot link data with a particular participant. The research participants should not be discussed beyond the needs of the project team, and the data must be kept secure at all times. This is particularly important with data stored on a computer. Access to the data should be restricted to only those people who have a legitimate reason to see it.

If confidentiality or anonymity cannot be guaranteed, participants must be warned in advance before they agree to participate. Confidentiality is a principle of research that is found in all professional codes and guidelines. If information needs to be disclosed in the public interest without a participant's consent, there must be a benefit to the individual or society that outweighs the individual's right to confidentiality. Researchers need to abide with the requirements of the law including the Data Protection Act 1998, the Health and Social Care Act 2001, and the Public Interest Disclosure Act 1998 which defines a public disclosure as where in good faith an employee reasonably believes:

- a criminal offence has been committed, is being committed, or is likely to be committed
- a person has failed, is failing, or is likely to fail to comply with any legal obligation to which they are subject
- a miscarriage of justice has occurred, is occurring or is likely to occur
- the health or safety of an individual has been, is being, or is likely to be endangered
- the environment has been, is being, or is likely to be damaged
- information related to any of the above has been, is being or is likely to be deliberately concealed.

Decisions about breaking confidentiality 'in the public interest' are complex with each case being considered on its merits as to whether the duty of confidence to the research participant should prevail over the disclosure of information.

The health and social care practitioner as data collector

Health and social care practitioners collecting data for research purposes must be as meticulous, accurate and reliable as they would be in collecting data in their normal work. There could be a conflict when a health and social care practitioner takes on a 'dual role' as practitioner and researcher. Practitioners working in this dual role must ensure that the data collected for research purposes is kept separate from patient information gathered in the daily work unless the research participant's consent is obtained. Practitioners must also be satisfied that any 'funded' research is ethically and scientifically sound and that, as individuals, they are not associated with any promotion of a particular product.

Health and social care practitioners must always uphold the principles of their own codes of conduct. They should possess the relevant research skills and knowledge compatible with the demands of the proposed research and acknowledge any limitations of their ability. As previously highlighted in an earlier chapter, a health and social care practitioner who is undertaking research must be certain that the knowledge sought is not already available.

Research Ethics Committees

Before researchers start their research project, they need to seek an independent ethical review of their proposed research. There are formalised procedures for researchers seeking ethical approval for research which involves clients and patients; access to notes and records; access to staff within health and social services; and access to premises within health and social care. In the case of health research, a NHS **Research Ethics Committee** will scrutinise research applications and make opinions as to whether the proposed research has considered all ethical issues.

For research involving a number of different NHS Trusts, there are arrangements for the research to be considered by a Multi-Centre Research Ethics Committee (MREC). Social services departments may also use a NHS Research Ethics Committee, or a University Ethics Committee or their own committee in order to seek an independent ethical review of any proposed research which falls into their sphere of responsibility.

Ethics committees are likely to follow the principles outlined earlier in this chapter in order to review potential research projects. Membership of the committee is multi-professional with members having experience across all types of research design. Lay people are also likely to be members, and they will be able to give the perspective of an ordinary individual who is not in professional practice. Ethical review involves an application form, a research protocol that provides details of the proposed research, copies of the research instruments (for example, questionnaires, interview schedules) and most importantly participant information sheets and consent forms. Some committees require the researchers to attend a committee meeting to answer questions about the proposed work, and a researcher may not commence their research until the Research Ethics Committee has given a favourable opinion.

Research Governance

In addition to gaining a favourable opinion following an independent ethical review, researchers conducting research in health and social services need to have their research approved by the NHS Trust(s) or social service department(s) where they wish to conduct their research. This requires them to satisfy the NHS Trust/social service department that the research has fulfilled a number of research governance requirements. These are:

- high scientific quality
- peer review
- identified sponsor (usually the employer of the lead researcher)
- financial probity
- adequate monitoring
- involvement of users of the research
- sufficient indemnity and compensation
- evidence of independent ethical review.

Research governance has come about as a result of a number of high profile research scandals and increasing public awareness of ethical issues.

Key Points

- Health and social care practitioners must be aware of ethical issues when they are reading research.
- Informed consent is an important consideration in all research involving human participants.
- Some research participants, such as children and people with a mental health problem, are considered vulnerable.
- Confidentiality and anonymity should be maintained.
- Research Ethics Committees and research governance procedures serve the interests of patients with regard to research.

Further Reading

Central Office for Research Ethics Committees: www.corec.org.uk

General Medical Council (2002). *Research: the role and responsibilities of doctors* www.gmc-uk.org/guidance/library/index (accessed 19.12.05).

Royal College of Nursing Research Society (2005). *Informed consent in health and social care research* www.rcn.org.uk/publications (accessed 19.12.05).

Soteriou, T. and Hek, G. (2003). Research governance and students: what are NHS Trusts looking for? *Nurse Researcher, 11* (1), 22–31.

Available on the HMSO Website: www.hmso.gov.uk/acts

Data Protection Act 1998
Health and Social Care Act 2001
Human Rights Act 1998
Public Interest Disclosure Act 1998

11 Critical Appraisal of Health and Social Care Research

Learning Outcomes

On completion of this chapter the reader should be able to:

- appreciate the need to critically appraise research and evidence
- identify the strengths and weaknesses of qualitative and quantitative research
- critically appraise a research journal article.

Key Terms

- critical appraisal   ■ critiquing framework

Introduction

Individuals working in a health and social care setting need to be able to critically appraise research for many different reasons. In Chapter 1 the term 'research literate' was used as a basis for discussion. This discussion centred on the need to be able to appreciate the skills and knowledge required to understand and use research to provide a high quality service. A result of having these skills and knowledge is the ability to be able to read and critically appraise the many research articles in journals.

We use evaluative and critical skills in our everyday life. Every time a decision is made in the supermarket regarding the brand of toothpaste or shampoo we buy, we are influenced by sources, such as marketing, the media, our experiences, family tradition, the cost. So these skills are not new but they do need to be developed to be applied to the world of research. Before critically appraising research it is important to recognise that this does not necessarily mean being negative. Critical appraisal, sometimes referred to as critiquing, is more about looking for strengths and weaknesses in a study and making a balanced judgement about what has been presented in the publication. Crookes and Davies (1998) discuss the term critic and conclude that to be critical means to make a judgement of the value or worth of a piece of literature or art, and it is in this context that critically appraising research should be considered.

Developing critical appraisal skills has become crucial to all professionals and students regardless of their working background. Many courses ask for a research critique or demonstration of critical appraisal skills within their assessment schemes. Some institutions of higher education include a literature review in their dissertation assessment which will require critically appraising many pieces of research in trying to answer a research question. Acquiring the skills needed to critically appraise published research depends on practice and thoughtful reading of research articles and reports. At first the language can appear alien, and sometimes the results appear to be written in a format requiring high levels of statistical knowledge to interpret. This may leave the reader feeling bewildered.

A worthwhile introduction to reading research and developing critical appraisal skills is to read several research articles which all address the same (or similar) topic. This topic should be one in which the reader is particularly interested either for an assignment or because they feature a specific subject. It is surprising how an interest in a specific subject helps overcome some of the immediate challenges of reading research. The other point to recognise is that not all parts of the research paper need be understood in the first couple of readings. However, gradually, as knowledge is increased, more and more will be understood. A common approach described by LoBiondo-Wood and Haber (1998) is to read an article at least four times, and each time read the article in a slightly different way (see Appendix 3) to gain a good understanding of the research.

In the final stages of reading a research article various questions can be asked at each stage of the research process. This helps identify both strengths and weaknesses of the study; it also breaks down the task into 'manageable chunks'. The rest of this chapter looks at various parts of the research process and identifies areas that the reader could question. A critical appraisal framework is found in Appendix 1.

Setting the research scene

In the first part of the article the author should identify the purpose of the study and why the research needs to be completed. This might be because a problem was identified or the researcher had a question they wanted to answer. Whatever the reason, all research should contribute to knowledge, either by identifying more questions to ask or by adding findings to the current body of knowledge. There needs to be some reassurance from the research that the study will fulfil this requirement and that the researcher is appropriately prepared to be conducting the study. There should be a clear purpose for the research, with a researchable problem.

Unless the researcher has identified that they are using grounded theory and are purposely not looking at the related literature until later in the study, the literature review should provide a background to the study. In the literature review there should be a comparing and contrasting of the literature, and a critique of it rather than simply a description. The strengths and weaknesses of previous studies should be identified and the dates of the studies should be noted. Although the literature review should include any seminal work on the topic, regardless of its age, there should be an attempt to embrace the most recent work as well.

Developing from the background and literature review, the researcher should establish a focus for the study. In a quantitative study this should be a defined focus often in the form of a hypothesis but it might also be a question or an aim (see Chapter 6). If there is a hypothesis it should be seen to emerge from the literature and it must be relevant to the topic being studied. The wording of the hypothesis should be clear and at least two variables identified. It should also be obvious whether the researcher is looking for a relationship between two or more variables or for differences between groups. When appraising a quantitative report where a null hypothesis is tested, the reader should check to see whether a null hypothesis has been used and if the statistical analysis includes a two-tailed test of significance.

In qualitative studies there should be a focus for the study in the form of aims, questions or objectives. These can be scrutinised for their relevance to the research approach and the literature review. In both qualitative and quantitative studies the hypothesis, aims or objectives should be examined to see if they link the previous work completed in this topic area with the research about to be undertaken. By keeping this as a central focus when appraising a study the reader can often discover inconsistencies either with the literature and the approach or with the literature and the design. In order to do this the reader must be familiar with the purpose of research aims, hypotheses and questions.

Collecting the data and sample selection

One of the ways the researcher can demonstrate their creativity is in the design of their study. There should be some indication of how they decided on their eventual research design – the influences and the constraints. The researcher should be able to demonstrate that the chosen design is appropriate to the study. For example, Preston (1997) used observations in her study of how families of patients with coronary artery disease used health promotion information. An alternative might have been to interview people and ask them how they used the information. However, the researcher recognised that there may be a difference between what people say they do and how they actually behave. Therefore, interviewing respondents could be seen as an inappropriate research design in this instance.

The heart of critical appraisal lies in an analysis of the way in which data were collected to solve the research problem. Therefore, in any research critique there should be an examination of alternative strategies to the one presented. Once the design has been examined the data collection methods and the sample used need careful scrutiny. The appropriate size of the sample will differ depending on the research approach used. In qualitative studies a small sample is used to gain in-depth information. Even with a small sample, the selection of individuals for the sample should be justified by the researcher. In qualitative studies the researcher might focus on particular respondents because of a specific interest. Particularly in a grounded theory approach the researcher will look at the early data received and use that to guide where they go for subsequent data. This should be explained and rationalised in the study.

When critically appraising deductive studies the reader should examine the sample very carefully. The whole thrust of studies which attempt to test a theory using a quantitative data collection method is the transfer of the results from the sample to the research population. In an attempt to eradicate bias the researcher should strive to use a random sample in which everyone in the research population has an equal chance of being included. As most research studies have constraints on them in terms of cost, a totally randomised sample is rarely seen in health and social care research. However, the implications of how the sample was selected should be included and allowed for in any discussion of the results and attempts at generalising the results. The sample should also mimic the research population in terms of its constitution. A quick look at a research study to see how the sample and research population match up in their constituent parts will give the reader an insight into the research. A researcher can only generalise to a research population that matches the sample group. When examining how the sample was selected, it is also important to examine how the participants were recruited and how they gave informed consent. There may have been a difference in the participants who participated and those who declined to participate or were not selected.

The data collection method should be described as well as rationalised. There may be an example of the data collection tool in the article and this allows for an examination of the questionnaire or interview schedule. Any measuring tool should also be included along with a discussion on how it was tested for reliability and validity and how the individuals collecting the data were trained in its use. At this point in the study there might be a description of the pilot study. This should indicate any changes made to the data collection tool and identify any problems the researcher found with the research design. It can take some honesty for the research to identify such problems. If results of the pilot study are not given, the reader is left unsure of what was found and somewhat insecure of the data collection methods used.

When evaluating a questionnaire there needs to be an examination of the types of questions used and their relevance to the approach taken. A qualitative approach will require the interviewer to use open questions, which allow the respondent to explain exactly how they feel/think. The closed questions and measuring scales found in quantitative studies should be examined for their ease of use, their clarity and the clarity of the instructions given for their use. All questions should give respondents an opportunity to add any other thoughts they might have on the subject. In observational studies there should be some indication of the role of the observer and whether it was covert or overt observation and whether the researcher included the effect of researcher presence on any results. The researcher should also detail how the field notes were recorded and when full notes were written up.

Results and data analysis

Possibly the one aspect that many individuals feel least able to critically appraise is the result and analysis section of a research study. The first area that needs to be examined is the relevance of the results to the research approach taken. If an inductive (qualitative) approach was taken the results section should demonstrate the emergence of themes from the data. Results should not necessarily offer an explanation but may simply give the reader the findings. In such research reports the researcher should indicate how the results were authenticated. This might involve triangulation when two methods could be used to collect the same information, for example, in-depth interviews and observations of behaviour or the data may be returned to participants. In the search for themes from qualitative data a colleague might be asked to identify themes from a sample of the responses to see if there is agreement or participants might be involved in validating any emerging themes. The steps that have been taken to demonstrate the trustworthiness of the data in a qualitative study should be clear.

If a deductive (quantitative) approach was taken in which the variables were measured, the results section should give the full range of responses. The beginning of the section should also identify the response rate from any questionnaires used. A description of the results might include pictorial representation, such as pie or bar charts, tables or graphs. These can help the reader get an overview of the results. However, all sections of any diagrams need to be accurately labelled otherwise the reader is left trying to guess what is being referred to. The diagrams should also be clear and able to 'stand alone'. If they require text to explain them they are usually inadequate.

In deductive analysis the researcher should justify the use of specific statistical tests. The reader should be able to see a clear link between the research approach, the level of measurement gained from the data collection tool and the statistical tests used. The level of significance produced by the statistical testing should also be examined to ensure it is above the 5% ($p < 0.05$) level. In health and social care research if there is a greater than 5% probability that the results occurred by chance they are usually deemed non-significant (see Chapter 9).

Conclusions and discussion of results

One of the dangers in any research report is that the researcher will attribute more meaning to the results than the analysis will support. In moving from the data analysis section to the interpretation and conclusions the reader should be able to follow a logical progression. Any generalisation made by the researcher should be examined in the light of the results section and (if it is a qualitative study) the sample used. One of the most frequently seen problems with research is that of a small sample used in a quantitative study. For example, following statistical testing and finding significant results the researcher 'ignores' the size and constitution of the sample. The researcher need not be criticised for using a small sample but can be challenged for generalising the results from the sample to the research population without acknowledging the limitations of the study.

If the research has a hypothesis, the interpretation of the results should be examined in the light of it. The hypothesis should be accepted or rejected. The data may or may not support the hypothesis. Remember nothing in research is ever proven (see Chapter 6) as there is always an element of chance in the results, or an error in the data collection methods.

Health and social care research should always address any implications for practice and policy. Ultimately research is about adding to a body of knowledge and that might be about, for example, the individuals who decide to be social workers or it may be about patients' perceptions of the physiotherapy treatment they receive. There should always be an identifiable link between the research undertaken and its practical application.

Key points

- It is essential that all health and social care workers develop critical appraisal skills.
- In order to understand research papers it is necessary to read them several times.
- All readers of research should use a systematic framework to appraise research papers.

Further Reading

Atkins, J. M. (1998). Evidence based health care: the role of the Cochrane collaboration. *British Journal of Therapy and Rehabilitation, 5* (5), 261–265.

Greenhalgh, T. (1997). *How to read a paper.* London: BMJ Publishing group.

Gomm, R., Needham, G. and Bullman, A. (Eds.) (2000). *Evaluating research in health and social care.* London: Open University Press and Sage Publications.

Muir Gray, J. (1997). *Evidence-based health care.* New York: Churchill Livingstone.

12 Disseminating and Implementing Research

Learning Outcomes

On completion of this chapter the reader should be able to:

- recognise and appreciate the need for the dissemination of research in the health and social care professions
- identify mechanisms for dissemination of research in health and social care
- appreciate some of the problems of research utilisation in the health and social care professions
- acknowledge the responsibilities of practitioners with regard to the implementation of research as an element of evidence-based practice.

Key Terms

■ research dissemination ■ evidence-based practice ■ research implementation ■ research utilisation

Introduction

In this book, we have constantly highlighted the need for practitioners to recognise the importance of using research in their daily practice. We have used the now common term 'research literacy' to describe the skills that health and social care practitioners need to enable them to gain access to relevant literature, and to be able to read and critically appraise research and other types of evidence. In developing these skills, practitioners will be able to assess the appropriateness of utilising research-based evidence in their daily practice in order to provide the highest standards of care possible. In addition, they will be able to contribute to the identification of research problems and priorities that may need to be further investigated.

Finding out about research that is relevant to practice is dealt with partly by thorough literature searching (see Chapter 4), and appraising it for quality is dealt with in Chapter 11. This chapter deals with the final stage of the research process – dissemination – and explores the ways in which researchers disseminate their work, and then considers the complex issue of the research–practice gap, research–application and implementation.

Dissemination of research

There is widespread recognition of the need for research findings to be disseminated effectively. Researchers have a responsibility to ensure that their research findings are appropriately disseminated in different forms and at different stages to address the needs of different people. These may include fellow practitioners, academic colleagues, researchers, policy-makers, and most importantly, the participants. Disseminating findings to participants might include feedback to local groups, summaries of findings to individuals, or writing an article for a magazine that service users might read.

In some types of research, for example, feminist research or action research, the commitment to disseminate and implement is much greater as this is part of the philosophy underpinning the research design and will be an important part of the research process. Those who are most able to act on the research findings in some way are likely to be practitioners, policy-makers, and perhaps the academic community through teaching students. Researchers, therefore, need to disseminate their work in places relevant to these groups and in a format likely to be of use.

One of the most common places for the dissemination of research findings is through journals as they can normally publish research within a year or two whereas a published book will take longer. Much quicker, however, is the presentation of findings at major conferences that are usually organised for specific audiences, such as sports physiotherapists, neonatal nurses, diagnostic radiographers; or on a particular topic for a multi-professional audience, such as community rehabilitation services, child protection developments, advances in diabetes. Other means of dissemination might be through continuing professional development activity, local conferences, newsletters and web pages, feedback and audit mechanisms, or through summaries of findings.

Ethical issues might arise for the researcher wanting to publish findings that may be controversial or negative, and they will need to consider the consequences of publishing or not in terms of the ethical principles identified in Chapter 10. Researchers also have a responsibility to clearly identify the implications of their research, particularly where related to practice, and many professional journals ask that this is made explicit for the readers.

The Cochrane Collaboration based in Oxford was set up in 1992, and has been established to provide information about existing research evidence. It produces the Cochrane Library, which is a main source of information to aid dissemination; it is primarily an international network of people who prepare, maintain and disseminate systematic up-to-date reviews of the effectiveness of health care. A sister organisation, the Campbell Collaboration, produces reviews relevant to social interventions. These are all provided electronically through databases and on the internet to make dissemination as easy as possible. The Centre for Reviews and Dissemination (CRD) at York also provides a service disseminating reviews of effectiveness to key decision-makers in the health service. The National Institute for Health and Clinical Excellence (NICE) produces and disseminates evidence-based clinical guidelines for health care, and the Social Care Institute for Excellence (SCIE) disseminates information about particular areas of social care. Both are extensive and free online resources with publications that can be downloaded or provided as hard copies.

A second key development in social care is the commitment from Barnardo's, the UK's largest childcare charity, to support evidence-based practice. This is demonstrated through the publication of a series of overviews on evidence of the effectiveness of interventions in the area of childcare called 'What works?' Barnardo's also produce briefing documents and have funded a series of workshops for social care practitioners specifically around the use of evidence in practice.

Implementation

There is a whole body of literature demonstrating that research has had minimal impact on practice, for example, Nutley and Davies (2000). Many have explored the reasons why it is so difficult to implement research findings when there is strong evidence to support a change in practice. Some of the focus of this has been on the different interests and concerns of researchers and practitioners, and the resulting difficulty communicating effectively. Other practical reasons cited by practitioners as barriers to implementation include: not having time and permission to read; not working in a culture where debate, reflection and critical awareness are encouraged; not having access to readable material; not having journals and libraries as part of the work environment; and not having a culture that embraces change. Furthermore, in some areas, the debate about 'what counts as evidence' can have a powerful effect on whether research gets into practice.

Macguire (1990) considers a number of different levels at which the implementation of research needs to be thought about, and she examines the uptake of research findings as a consideration within the overall management of change. She says how important it is not to blame any one group, for example, practitioners, researchers, policy-makers; and suggests that the integration of research and practice has to be confronted at all levels within an organisation. Nutley and Davies (2000) identify a number of strategies that have been used for changing individual and organisation practice. These include strategies aimed at individual professionals, such as opinion leaders; production of educational material; strategies aimed at organisations through reorganising skill mix; developing multi- disciplinary teams; regulatory interventions; financial interventions; and patient- orientated interventions, such as involving patients and clients in decision-making. Other strategies to encourage research implementation might include joint appointments across research and practice, and practice appointments with a research component, for example, consultant nurses, consultant physiotherapists.

It is clear that the dissemination and implementation of research is a complex phenomenon and changing practice requires more than just the dissemination of findings. However, practitioners are a powerful group who have a responsibility to consider both the ways in which evidence can make a difference to the care of their clients and patients, and how a change in practice might be made. New ways of implementing research into everyday work are now being considered including: the development of integrated care pathways, quality improvement processes, auditing techniques, and computer support systems. Research is being conducted to identify how effective different approaches to implemention might be in terms of changing the behaviour of health and social care professionals. A key message from all the work in this area is that single interventions do not work as well as multifaceted interventions, and that there needs to be understanding about individual decision-making and behavioural change in order to effectively get research into practice.

Key Points

- Research findings need to be effectively disseminated by researchers.
- Implementation of research findings can be challenging and various strategies can be used to change practice.
- All health and social care practitioners have a responsibility to utilise research based evidence in their practice.

Further Reading

Bassett, B. (Ed.) (2001). *Implementing research in the clinical setting.* London: Whurr Publishers.

Davies, H.T.O., Nutley, S. M. and Smith, P.C. (2000). *What Works?* Bristol: The Policy Press.

Jackson, S. and Thomas, N. (1999). *What works in maintaining stability in care?* Barkingside: Barnardo's.

Appendix I   Critical Appraisal Framework

The purpose of the study

- Is the knowledge sought already available?
- Is there an important reason for the research to be undertaken?
- Are the potential outcomes of the study realistic?
- Was the researcher(s) appropriately qualified/supported to undertake the research?
- Are there any concerns about any funders of the research in relation to the process of the research described?

Research problem and research questions

- Is the problem significant and researchable and have all potential ways of solving the problem been considered?
- Are all research questions and hypotheses developed directly from the problem?
- Did the research place unethical or unrealistic demands on participants?

Literature search

- Was there a search of a good range of literature?
- Was there a search strategy with named databases and key search terms?
- Was the review balanced and not biased?
- Was the literature critically appraised?
- Was any conflicting evidence clearly presented?
- Did the literature review provide rationale and direction for the research?
- Were any limitations of the literature identified?

Sample selection

- Was an appropriate sampling strategy used?
- If a random sample was selected, was it genuinely random?
- Were any biases in the sample group identified?

- Was the target population identified in a quantitative study?
- Was there a clear account of how participants were recruited and selected to take part in the study?
- Was there any coercion in recruiting participants?
- Was there clear evidence that participants gave informed consent?
- If the participants were vulnerable, has this been clearly considered in the study?
- Was the research reviewed by a Research Ethics Committee?
- Were any governance issues dealt with appropriately?
- Were all the participants accounted for throughout the study, i.e, did the numbers add up?

Research design and data collection

- Was the design of the study appropriate to the research questions?
- Was an appropriate method of data collection used?
- Were the participants protected from physical and psychological harm?
- Was the issue of 'deception' dealt with appropriately in observational studies?
- Were the data gathered by appropriate people?
- Was the researcher's role and relationship with the participants fully considered?
- Were the data authenticated in qualitative studies?

Results and analysis of findings

- Were the results and analysis linked back to the original research question?
- Were the results and analysis manipulated in order to favour particular findings?
- Was there any evidence of lost data?
- Was there evidence of a statistician's input into complex quantitative analysis?

Conclusions, recommendations and limitations

- Were the conclusions and recommendations based on the results of the study?
- Was it clear that there was no intention to mislead or give false conclusions?
- Was the sample selected considered in relation to the recommendations?
- Did the researcher acknowledge any limitations?
- Were limitations of the findings of the study identified, as well as limitations of the study design and techniques?

General points including ethical issues

- Ethical issues should be considered at all stages of the study.
- There should be clear evidence that privacy, dignity, anonymity and confidentiality were maintained throughout the study.
- The researcher should have identified ethical issues related to the study.
- The researcher should acknowledge sources of support and funding.
- When critically appraising research, readers should acknowledge their own limitations and gain assistance when necessary.

Appendix 2 Literature Searching

Sources of research literature

- Systematic reviews are really important sources of research literature on a specific topic. The Cochrane Library (www.cochrane.org.uk) is the best source of systematic reviews on health care effectiveness and the Social Care Institute of Excellence www.scie.org.uk produces reviews that evaluate existing research and literature about particular aspects of health care.
- Journals that contain comprehensive research articles such as: *British Journal of Addiction, British Journal of Learning Disabilities, British Journal of Therapy and Rehabilitation, Journal of Family Therapy, Health and Social Care in the Community, Radiology, Physiotherapy, Social Work Research, Journal of Advanced Nursing, Intensive and Critical Care Nursing, Journal of Clinical Nursing.*
- Journals that specialise in reviewing research such as: *Clinical Evidence, Effective Health Care Bulletins, Evidence-based Health Care, Evidence-based Mental Health, Evidence-based Nursing, Journal of Clinical Effectiveness, Journal of Social Service Research.*
- Published research reports and reviews from various organisations such as: government departments, professional bodies, university departments (e.g., University of York Social Policy Research Unit), research units, specialist units, reports for the funders of research (e.g., Health Technology Assessment), charities and voluntary organisations (e.g., Joseph Rowntree Foundation Reports).
- Conference papers that have been produced as a result of a national or international conference and put into a single document.
- Specialist books that report research studies on a specific subject topic. Usually the books are edited and each chapter has a different author who has undertaken research in the subject area.
- Theses and dissertations that are produced as the result of research undertaken for a degree. These are usually available at the university where the degree was undertaken and can be borrowed for a short while, either fully bound or as a micro-fiche.

Other useful information resources

- Online and CD-ROM databases that can be used to search for research and evidence such as: Allied and Alternative Medicine (AMED), CANCERLIT, Cumulative Index to Nursing and Allied Health Literature (CINAHL), Cochrane Library, MEDLINE, National Research Register (NRR), psychology and related disciplines (PsycLIT), grey literature (SIGLE), Caredata, International Bibliography of Social Science, National Electronic Library for Health, AgeInfo, MIDIRS, ChildData, Applied Social Sciences Index and Abstracts (ASSIA).
  Internet resources – there are many internet sites, many acting as gateways to the large amount of information available. Local health and social care libraries will be able to give up-to-date information, for example:

  http://www.omni.ac.uk
  http://www.shef.ac.uk/~scharr/ir/netting.html
  http://www.sosig. ac.uk/

- The King's Fund Library which is concerned with health care and organisational management.
- National Institute for Health and Clinical Excellence (NICE) for clinical guidelines, technology appraisals and public health guidance.
- The Nuffield Institute for Health Information Resource Centre keeps a database called Health Management Information Service (HELMIS).
- The Centre for Reviews and Dissemination (CRD) at York keeps a database of good quality research reviews of the effectiveness and cost-effectiveness of health care interventions, and the management and organisation of health services. It also keeps a database of published economic evaluations of health care interventions.

Appendix 3 Four Stages in Critical Appraisal

There are four stages in the critical appraisal of a study (LoBiondo-Wood and Haber, 1998):

1 A quick skim read to familiarise yourself with the study.
2 Skilled reading to understand the different parts of the study in relation to the whole.
3 Each part of the study is broken down and appraised in terms of its scientific merit and use to health and social care professionals.
4 All parts are reconstituted into a whole. The reader decides how each stage of the research process is addressed and then considers the overall impact of the study.

Glossary

Abstract

a brief summary of a piece of research which identifies the main stages of the research process.

Action research

an approach to research which attempts to bring about change as a result of reflection on practice. The researcher works alongside practitioners in order to effect change.

Anonymity

ensuring non-identification of research subjects or organisations, so that they cannot be linked with the data being collected.

Bias

an unintentional influence or effect which may occur at any stage of the research process and which distorts the findings, e.g., sample bias, interview bias.

Bibliographic database

databases held on CD-ROMS or computers that contain details of publications, e.g., CINAHL, MEDLINE, ASSIA.

Case study

in-depth study of an individual or organisation or event.

Cochrane library

an electronic library of databases which include systematic reviews of the effectiveness of health care.

Common sense

knowledge that is commonly accepted.

Concept

an abstract idea which may be informed by previous experience or knowledge.

Confidentiality

ensuring data are used only for the purpose for which they are gathered and that information gathered cannot be linked to an individual.

Content analysis

the processing and interpretation of non-numerical data, e.g., examining text in great depth for recurring words or themes.

Control group	subjects that do not receive an intervention or treatment in an experiment.
Correlation coefficient	a figure calculated to demonstrate the size and direction of relationship between two variables.
Critical appraisal	identifying the strengths and weaknesses of evidence by systematically considering the research processes, and making judgements about relevance and application to practice.
Data analysis	the processing, summarising and interpretation of raw data into meaningful information.
Deductive	a process by which general principles or theories are applied to a particular situation.
Delphi technique	a technique for gathering views or opinions or judgements from a group of experts.
Dependent variable	the variable that is observed as the *effect* of manipulation by an independent variable.
Descriptive statistics	the use of various statistical techniques to describe numerical data, e.g., mean, standard deviation, variance.
Dissemination	ensuring the results of research are communicated to a wide audience.
Evaluation research	investigating how a policy or new practice is working.
Ethnography	a research approach which usually involves the researcher studying individuals or groups in their natural setting.
Evidence-based practice	practice that is based on current best evidence, professional expertise and experience, and the patients' preference.
Experiment	a scientific research design which tests a hypothesis and whereby subjects are randomly allocated to different groups (see: control group; experimental group).
Experimental group	subjects that receive an intervention or treatment in an experiment.
External validity	the extent to which findings can be generalised to other populations or situations.

Feminist research	a particular research approach which seeks to empower women.
Gatekeeper	a term often used to describe a person or persons who are attempting to safeguard the interests of others.
Generalisability	the degree to which the researcher can transfer research findings from the studied sample to a target population.
Grounded theory	a qualitative approach to research which uses the process of inductive reasoning to develop theory from specific observations.
Historical research	research that aims to discover facts and understand past events.
Hawthorne effect	an effect which occurs as a result of subjects knowing they are involved in a study.
Hypothesis	a measurable statement which sets out the expected relationship between two or more variables.
Implementation	the development of techniques to promote and support the utilisation of research.
Independent variable	in experimental research, the independent variable is the variable that is manipulated, and is thought to be the *cause* (in a cause and effect relationship).
Inductive	a process by which principles or theories are developed from a particular situation or observation.
Inferential statistics	the use of various statistical techniques either to infer meaning from the sample to the target population or to demonstrate the strength of a relationship between variables.
Informed consent	obtaining verbal or written permission from an individual to voluntarily take part in a study.
Interviews	a data collection technique that involves gathering information through verbal communication, often using a schedule, e.g., telephone interviewing, one-to-one interviews, group interviews.
Intuition	insight that is developed through experience.

Likert scale	a refined measurement scale that requires the respondent to give opinion on a series of statements.
Literature review	a section of a report, or a whole report where previous research or literature on a specific subject has been evaluated or appraised.
Literature search	systematic and through exploration of literature (e.g., journal articles, books, reports) on a specific subject.
Longitudinal study	a study by which the same subjects are studied at different points over a period of time.
Mean	the arithmetic average of a set of scores.
Median	the mid-point in a set of ranked scores.
Medical model	approach to health care which is derived from medical knowledge and practice.
Meta-analysis	a statistical technique which summarises results from several studies into a single estimate.
Mixed-methods	using different data collection methods in addressing research questions within one study, often including qualitative and quantitative methods.
Mode	the most frequently occurring characteristic in a data set. Where *two* characteristics occur most frequently, the term bi-modal is used.
Non-parametric tests	a group of statistical tests used to identify differences or relationships between variables. Suitable for ordinal or nominal data.
Non-participant observation	a technique for gathering observational data where the researcher is detached from the situation being studied.
Non-probability sample	the researcher is unable to state the statistical likelihood of a member of the target population appearing in the sample. The selection of the samples was by non-random techniques.
Null hypothesis	a statement that predicts that there will be no relationship between identified variables. Sometimes known as a statistical hypothesis.

Observation	a data collection technique that involves gathering information through visual means, e.g., watching, sometimes using a schedule to record the observations.
Parametric tests	a group of sensitive and powerful statistical tests used to identify differences or relationships between variables and which are applied to interval or ratio levels of measurement.
Participant observation	a technique for gathering observational data where the researcher is part of the situation being studied.
Phenomenon	an event studied by the researcher.
Phenomenology	a research approach which examines the lived experiences of individuals from their own perceptions.
Pilot study	a small preliminary study that allows the researcher to test the research methodology, e.g. data collection techniques.
Probability	the likelihood of research findings occurring by chance, which may be identified by a p value.
Probability sample	a sample selected randomly, allowing the researcher to state the statistical likelihood of a member of the target population appearing in the sample.
Qualitative data analysis	processing and interpretation of non-numerical data, e.g., words and text.
Qualitative data collection	gathering non-numerical data such as words and text, through various techniques, e.g., interviews and observations.
Quantitative data analysis	processing and interpretation of numerical data.
Quantitative data collection	gathering primarily numerical data through various techniques, e.g., structured questionnaires, measuring scales, physiological measurements.
Quasi-experiment	an experiment-like study which is not able to conform to all the requirements of an experiment.

Questionnaire	a data collection instrument composed of written questions that require written responses.
Randomised controlled trial	an experiment conducted in a practice environment.
Raw data	before any processing, the information that has been systematically collected by the researcher.
Reflective practice	systematically looking back and learning from past practice and experience.
Reliability	the extent to which an instrument or technique shows consistency of measurement.
Repertory grid	a technique used to elicit perceptions.
Replication	repeating another researcher's study using the same techniques as in the original research.
Representative sample	the degree to which a sample has the characteristics of the research population.
Research Ethics Committee	an independent group of people who meet regularly with a common aim of judging the appropriateness and scientific merit of proposed research.
Research Governance	procedures for ensuring that research conducted within the health and social services is of high scientific quality, is properly managed, has the interests of service users, has had an independent ethical review, and is appropriately monitored.
Research question	a specific question that the researcher is seeking the answer to through investigation.
Retrospective study	examining data that have been collected in the past. It is often used for the purpose of establishing a relationship between variables.
Rituals	routine and unquestioned actions.
Sample	a portion or part of a population, from which data can be collected.
Sampling	the techniques used to select a portion or part of a population.
Sampling bias	over- or under-representation of characteristics of the target population found in the sample.

Sampling error	problems resulting from the sampling technique, which lead to the generation of a biased sample.
Sampling frame	a record of all members of the population from which a sample can be selected.
Scientific knowledge	knowledge verified by systematic and rigorous enquiry.
Search strategy	the method used for searching for evidence/research to answer a particular question.
Secondary data	the extraction and use of data that have been previously collected for another purpose, e.g., hospital admission rates.
Sources of knowledge	different types of knowledge that can be used as a basis for decision-making.
Standard deviation	a figure calculated to identify the spread of the data set around the mean.
Statistical significance	the extent to which results are 'real' rather than due to chance.
Systematic literature review	a systematic process of locating, critically appraising and synthesising literature with the aim of producing an overview.
Tacit knowledge	developed thorough the experience of practice over a period of time, part of 'expert opinion'.
Target population	the entire membership of the group in which the researcher is interested and from which data can be collected.
Theory	a structured collection of ideas or concepts which seeks to explain or describe phenomena.
Tradition	continued use of past actions or customs which may or may not have lost their meaning.
Trial and error	trying different ways of solving a problem until a solution is found.
Triangulation	the use of two or more research approaches, data collection methods or analysis techniques in the same study.
Trustworthiness	a term used when appraising qualitative research when describing credibility, dependability and transferability.

Utilisation	the use and application of research findings to inform decision-making and practice.
Validity	the extent to which an instrument or technique measures what it is intended to measure.
Variable	a characteristic that varies between individuals and can be measured or manipulated in the research, e.g., age, pain, height, gender.
Vignette	short description of a scenario, situation, case study or topic, which is used to prompt data collection.

References

Agan, D. (1987). Intuitive knowledge as a dimension of nursing. *Advanced Nursing Science, 10* (1), 63–70.

Argyris, L. and Schon, D. (1974). *Theory in practice*. San Francisco: Jossey Bass.

Bassett, C. (1994). Nurse teachers' attitudes to research: a phenomenological study. *Journal of Advanced Nursing, 19* (3), 585–592.

Beauregard, C. and Solomon, P. (2005). Understanding the experiences of HIV/AIDS for women: implications for occupational therapists. *Journal of Occupational Therapy, 72* (2), 113–120.

Bell, J. (2005). *Doing your research project: a guide for first time researchers in education, health and social science* (4th ed.). Buckingham: Open University Press.

Benner, P. (1984). *From novice to expert: excellence and power in clinical nursing practice*. Menlo Park, CA: Addison-Wesley.

Bergen, A. and While, A. (2000). A case for case studies exploring the use of the case study design in community nursing research. *Journal of Advanced Nursing, 31* (4), 926–934.

Blaxter, L., Hughes, C. and Tight, M. (1996). *How to research*. Buckingham: Open University Press.

Booth, S., Booth, A. and Falzon, L. (2003). The need for information and research skills training to support evidence-based social care: a literature review and survey. *Learning in Health and Social Care, 2* (4), 191–201.

Bowling, A. (2002). *Research methods in health* (2nd ed.). Buckingham: Open University Press.

Burnard, P. (1989). The sixth sense. *Nursing Times, 85* (50), 52–53.

Burns, R.B. (2000). *Introduction to research methods*. London: Sage.

Burns, N. and Grove, S. (1999*). Understanding nursing research* (2nd ed.). Philadelphia: W.B. Saunders and Company.

Burns, N. and Grove, S. (2005). *The practice of nursing research. Conduct, critique and utilization* (5th ed.). St. Louis, MO: Elsevier Saunders.

Coffey, A., Holbrook, B. and Atkinson, P. (1996). Qualitative data analysis: technique and representation. *Sociological Research Online, 1* (1). www.socresonline.org.uk/1/1/4.html top (accessed on 28.02.06).

Cook, J.A. and Fonow, M. (1986). Knowledge and women's interest: issues of epistemology and methodology in feminist sociological research. *Sociological Enquiry*, Winter, 2–29.

Cormack, D. (2000). *The research process in nursing* (4th ed.). Oxford: Blackwell Science.

Crookes, P.A. and Davies, S. (1998). *Research into practice*. London: Bailliere Tindall.

Davies, H.T.O., Nutley, S.M. and Smith, P.C (Eds.) (2000). *What Works? Evidence-based policy and practice in public services*. Bristol: The Policy Press.

Depoy, E. and Gitlin, L.N. (1994). *Introduction to research: multiple strategies for health and human services*. St. Louis, MO: Mosby.

Evans, S., Huxley, P., Webber, M., Katona, C., Gately, C., Mears, A., Medina, J., Pajak, S. and Kendall, T. (2005). The impact of 'statutory duties' on mental health social workers in the UK. *Health and Social Care in the Community, 13* (2), 141–154.

Farnell, S., Maxwell, L., Tan, S. Rhodes, A. and Philips, B. (2005). Temperature measurement: comparison of non-invasive methods used in adult critical care. *Journal of Critical Nursing, 14* (5), 632–639.

Fielding, N. (1993) Qualitative interviewing. In Gilbert, N. (Ed.) (1993) *Researching social life* (pp. 145–163). London: Sage.

Fielding, J. (2001a) Coding and managing data. In Gilbert, N. (Ed.) (2001) *Researching social life* (2nd ed.) (pp. 227–251). London: Sage.

Fielding, N. (2001b) Ethnography. In Gilbert, N. (Ed.) (2001). *Researching social life* (pp. 145–163) (2nd ed.). London: Sage.

Gibbs, G. (2002). *Qualitative data analysis explorations with Nvivo*. Buckingham: Open University Press.

Gilbert, N. (2001). *Researching social life* (2nd ed.). London: Sage.

Giles, H. and Moule, P. (2004). 'Do not attempt resuscitation' decision-making: a study exploring the attitudes and experiences of nurses. *Nursing in Critical Care, 9* (3), 115–122.

Glaser, B. and Strauss, A. (1967). *The discovery of grounded theory: strategies for qualitative research*. Chicago: Aldine.

Gomm, R., Hammersley, M. and Foster, P. (Eds.) (2000). *Case study method*. London: Sage.

Gray J. A. M. (1999). *Evidence-based healthcare: how to make health policy and management decisions*. London: Churchill Livingstone.

Greenwood, J. (1993). Reflective practice: a critique of the work of Argyris and Schon. *Journal of Advanced Nursing, 18* (8), 1183–1187.

Gunilla, C., Drew, N., Dahlberg, K. and Lutzen, K. (2002). Uncovering tacit caring knowledge. *Nursing Philosophy, 3* (20), 144–151.

Halford, K., Price, J., Kelly, A., Bouma, R. and Young, R. (2005). Helping the female partners of men abusing alcohol: a comparison of three treatments. *Addiction, 96* (10), 1497–1508.

Hanson, E.J. and Clarke, A. (2000). The role of telematics in assisting family carers and frail older people at home. *Health and Social Care in the Community, 8* (2), 129–137.

Haralambos, M., Holborn, M. and Heald, R. (2004). *Sociology, themes and perspectives* (6th ed.). London: Collins.

Hek, G., Langton, H. and Blunden, G. (2000). Systematically searching and reviewing literature. *Nurse Researcher, 7* (3), 40–57.

Hughes, R., Sinha, A., Higginson, I., Down, K. and Leigh, N. (2005). Living with motor neurone disease: lives, experiences of service and suggestions for change. *Health and Social Care in the Community*, *13* (1), 64–74.

Hsu, L. (2005). An exploratory study of Taiwanese consumers' experiences of using health-related websites. *Journal of Nursing Research*, *13* (2), 129–140.

Hung, C.-H. (2005). Measuring postpartum stress. *Journal of Advanced Nursing, 50* (4), 417–424.

Jacobson, A., Hamilton, P. and Galloway, J. (1993) Obtaining and evaluating secondary analysis in nursing research. *Western Journal of Nursing Research, 13* (4), 483–494.

Jegermalm, M. (2004). Informal care and support for carers in Sweden: patterns of service among informal carers and care recipients. *European Journal of Social Work, 7* (1), 7–24.

Karim, K. (2001). Assessing the strengths and weaknesses of action research. *Nursing Standard, 15* (26), 33–35.

Kealey, P. and McIntyre, I. (2005). An evaluation of domiciliary occupational therapy service in palliative cancer care in a community trust: a patient perspective. *European Journal of Cancer Care, 14* (3), 232–243.

Kent, P., Marks, D., Pearson, W. and Keating, S. (2005). Does clinician treatment choice improve the outcomes of manual therapy for non specific low backpain? A meta-analysis. *Journal of Manipulative and Physiological Therapeutics, 28* (5), 312–322.

Khan, K.S., Kunz, R., Kleijnen, J. and Antes, G. (2003). *Systematic reviews to support evidence-based medicine*. London: The Royal Society of Medicine Press Limited.

Kidder, L. and Judd, C. (1987). *Research methods in social relations* (5th ed.). New York: CBS Publishing.

Kirby, S. (2004). A historical perspective on the contrasting experiences of nurses as research subjects and research activists. *International Journal of Nursing Practice, 10* (6), 272–279.

Lincoln, Y. and Guba, Y. (1985). *Naturalistic enquiry*. Newbury Park: Sage.

LoBiondo-Wood, G. and Haber, J. (Eds.) (1998). *Nursing research: methods, critical appraisal and utilisation*. St. Louis MO: Mosby.

Macdonald, G. (2000). Social care: rhetoric and reality. In Davies, H.T.O., Nutley, S.M. and Smith, P.C. (Eds.), *What works? Evidence-based policy and practice in public services* (pp. 117–140). Bristol: The Policy Press.

Macguire, J.M. (1990). Putting nursing research findings into practice: research utilisation as an aspect of the management of change. *Journal of Advanced Nursing, 15* (5), 614–620.

Manias, E. and Street, A. (2001). Rethinking ethnography: reconstructing nursing relationships. *Journal of Advanced Nursing, 33* (2), 234–242.

Mason, C. (1993). Doing a research literature review. *Nurse Researcher, 1* (1), 43–55.

Mavundla, T. (2000). Professional nurses' perceptions of nursing mentally ill people in a general hospital setting. *Journal of Advanced Nursing, 32* (6), 1528–1569.

May, T. (1997). *Social research: issues, methods and process*. Buckingham: Open University Press.

Mizrahi, T. and Berger, C. (2001). Effect of a changing health care environment on social work leaders: obstacles and opportunities in hospital social work. *Social Worker, 46* (2), 170–182.

Moule, P. (2005). *E-learning for healthcare students: developing the communities of practice framework*. EdD thesis, University of the West of England, Bristol.

Needham, G. (2000). Accessing evidence: an overview of sources of information for evidence-based practice. In R. Gomm and C. Davies (Eds.), *Using Evidence in Health and Social Care* (pp. 233–248). London: Sage/Open University.

Neuman, W.L. (1994). *Social research methods: qualitative and quantitative approaches* (2nd ed.). London: Allyn and Bacon.

Ng, J., Sham, A., Tang, P. and Fung, S. (2004). SARS: pregnant women's fears and perceptions. *British Journal of Midwifery, 12* (11), 698–703.

National Institute for Health and Clinical Excellence (2003). Working together to prevent pressure ulcers. www.nice.org.uk (accessed on 10.12.05).

NHS Centre for Reviews and Dissemination (2001). *Undertaking systematic reviews of research on effectiveness: CRD report number 4* (2nd ed.). York: University of York, NHS CRD.

Nicolson, P., Burr, J. and Powell, J. (2005). Becoming an advanced practitioner in neonatal nursing: a psycho-social study of the relationship between educational preparation and role development. *Journal of Clinical Nursing, 14* (6), 727–738.

Nutley, S. and Davies, H. (2000). Making a reality of evidence-based practice. In H.T.O. Davies, S.M. Nutley and P.C. Smith (Eds.), *What Works? Evidence-based policy and practice in public services* (pp. 317–350). Bristol: The Policy Press.

Odd, D., Page, B., Battin, M. and Harding, J. (2004). Does radio-opaque contrast improve radiographic localisation of percutaneous central venous lines? *BMJ, 89* (1), F41-F43.

Oppenheim, A. (1992). *Questionnaire design, interviewing and attitude measurement* (2nd ed.). London: Pinter Publishers.

Panditi, S. and Silverman, M. (2003). Perception of exercise induced asthma by children and their parents. *Archives of Disease in Childhood, 88* (9), 807–811.

Payne, J. (2002). An action research project in a night shelter for rough sleepers. *Journal of Psychiatric and Mental Health Nursing, 9* (1), 95–101.

Perrotta, C., Ortiz, Z. and Rogue, M. (2005). *Chest physiotherapy for acute bronchiolitis in paediatric patients between 0 and 24 months old*. Oxford: The Cochrane Library.

Polit, D. and Beck, C. (2006). *Essentials of nursing research: methods, appraisal and utilization* (6th ed.). Philadelphia: Lippincott Williams and Wilkins.

Preston, R. (1997). Ethnography: studying the fate of health promotion in coronary families. *Journal of Advanced Nursing, 25* (4), 554–561.

Price, S. and Mitchell, M. (2004) Teenagers' experiences of the maternity services. *Evidence Based Midwifery, 2* (2), 66–70.

Pritchard, C. and Williams, R. (2001). A three year comparative longitudinal study of a school based social work family service to reduce truancy, delinquency and school exclusions. *Journal of Social Welfare and Family Law, 23* (1), 23–43.

Regehr, C. (2000). Action research: underlining or undermining the cause? *Social Work and Social Sciences Review, 8* (3), 194–206.

Resuscitation Council (UK) (2005). Guidelines for adult basic life support. www.resus.org.uk/pages/bls.pdf (accessed on 18.12.05).

Rew, L. and Sparrow, E. (1987) Intuition: a neglected hallmark of nursing knowledge. *Advances in Nursing Science, 10* (1), 49–62.

Reynolds, S. (2000). The anatomy of evidence-based practice: principles and methods. In L. Trinder and S. Reynolds (Eds.), *Evidence-based practice: a critical appraisal* (pp. 17–34). Oxford: Blackwell Science.

Robinson, L., Clare, L. and Evans, K. (2005). Making sense of dementia and adjusting to loss: psychological reactions to a diagnosis of dementia in couples. *Aging and Mental Health, 9* (4), 337–347.

Sackett, D.L., Richardson, W.S., Rosenburg, W. and Haynes, R.B. (1997). *Evidence-based medicine: how to practice and teach EBM.* London: Churchill Livingstone.

Scott, I. and Mazhindu, D. (2005). *Statistics for healthcare professionals.* London: Sage.

Schon, D. (1987). *Educating the reflective practitioner.* San Francisco: Jossey Bass.

Sofield, L. and Salmond, S. (2003). Workplace violence: a focus on verbal abuse and intent to leave the organization. *Orthopaedic Nursing, 22* (4), 274–283.

Spalding, N. (2004). Using vignettes to assist reflection within an action research study on a preoperative education programme. *British Journal of Occupational Therapy, 67* (9), 388–395.

Stark, S. (1994). Nurse tutors' experiences of personal and professional growth through action research. *Journal of Advanced Nursing, 19* (2), 342–348.

Strauss, A. and Corbin, J. (1997). *Grounded theory in practice.* Thousand Oaks: Sage.

Titchen, A. and Binnie, A. (1994). Action research: a strategy for theory generation and testing. *International Journal of Nursing Studies, 31* (1), 1–12.

Trinder, L. (2000a). The context of evidence-based practice. In L. Trinder and S. Reynolds (Eds.), *Evidence-based practice: a critical appraisal* (pp. 1–16). Oxford: Blackwell Science.

Trinder, L. (2000b). Evidence-based practice in social work and probation. In L. Trinder and S. Reynolds (Eds.), *Evidence-based practice: a critical appraisal* (pp. 138–162). Oxford: Blackwell Science.

Trinder, L. (2000c). A critical appraisal of evidence-based practice. In L. Trinder and S. Reynolds. (Eds.), *Evidence-based practice: a critical appraisal* (pp. 212–241). Oxford: Blackwell Science.

Trinder, L. and Reynolds, S. (Eds) (2000). *Evidence-based practice: a critical appraisal.* Oxford: Blackwell Science.

van der Lee, J.H., Wagenaar, R.C., Lankhorst, G.J., Vogelaar, T.W., Deville, W.I. and Bouter, L.M. (2000). Forced use of the upper extremity in chronic stroke patients: results from a single blind randomised clinical trial. *Stroke, 31* (40), 986–988.

van Manen, M. (1990). *Researching lived experience: human science for an action sensitive pedagogy.* London: Althouse Press.

Walsh, M. and Ford, P. (1989). *Nursing rituals: research and rational actions.* Oxford: Heinemann Nursing.

Walsh, M. and Ford, P. (1994). *New rituals for old: nursing through the looking glass.* Oxford: Heinemann.

Webb, C. (1993). Feminist research definitions, methodology, methods and evaluation. *Journal of Advanced Nursing, 18* (3), 416–423.

Welsh, I. and Lyons, C. (2001) Evidence-based care and the case for intuition and tacit knowledge in clinical assessment and decision-making in mental health nursing practice: an empirical contribution to the debate. *Journal of Psychiatric and Mental Health Nursing, 8* (4), 299–305.

White, J., Slabber, J. and Schreuder, A. (2001). Patient management: measuring patients' expectations and perceptions of service quality in a dental training hospital. *South African Dental Journal, 56* (4), 203–208.

Whitehead, D. (2005). Empirical or tacit knowledge as a basis for theory development? *Journal of Clinical Nursing, 14* (2), 143–144.

Whyte, J. 4th and Dawson, S. (2001). The sexual behaviours of African American women living with HIV disease: is perceived HIV status altering sexual behaviour? *Journal of the Association of Nurses in AIDS care, 12* (2), 56–65.

Yin, R. (1994). *Case study research: design and methods* (2nd ed.). Thousand Oaks: Sage.

Index